There is here with a T in front

A Collection of Perspectives

By Ron Colone

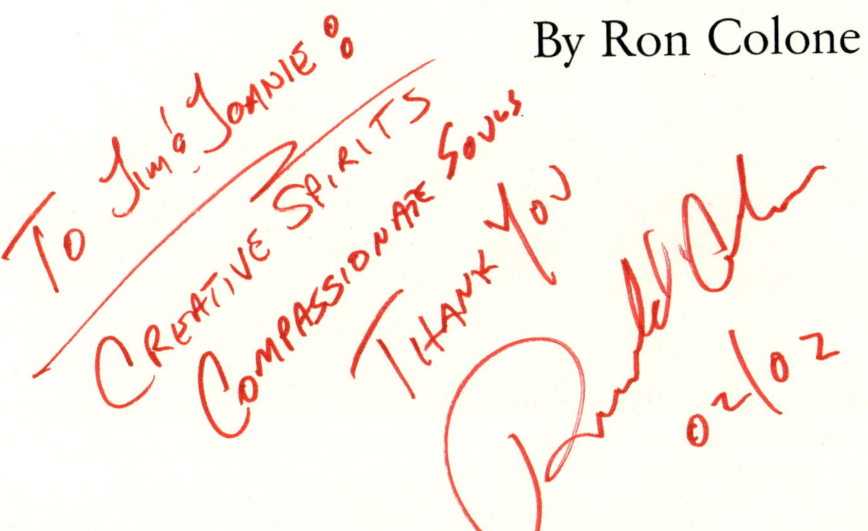

YMIOIMY
PO Box 1672
Santa Ynez, CA 93460
www.colone.org

**There is Here
with a T in Front**

Edited by Sterling Price
Cover photos by Henry Diltz

ISBN # 0-9672319-1-4
Library of Congress Catalog Card Number - pending
First Edition 2001

Printed in the United States of America

A note on the title

As I endeavored, through these writings, to broaden my horizons, I found that this *or* that became this *and* that, and that **There is Here – with a T in front.**

Also by Ron Colone

Communications: The Mechanics of Being
Twelve in a Tank
From the Backburner (poetry)
Fire Trails and Fire Tales
Collectives; A Collection of Perspectives

Thanks to the publisher, the staff and the readers of
The Santa Ynez Valley News

To my family

To Missy Collier,
Jeff Jurcisin,
Katie Fisher
and Jonathan King

To Sterling Price - whose influence as an editor has less to do with the writings in this book than with the writer that continues forth.

And especially to Kelly Elm -
for being a wall;
a wall that I lean against
a wall that holds things up
a wall that I bounce things off.

Grazie a Dio

Putting 'Perspective' in perspective

Dear Reader,

Whenever I see Ron Colone going by, he's usually on his way to something. Either he's coaching football at the high school or producing music shows, or bringing people together to have dinner and talk and get to know each other. He likes that ... I can tell 'cause he gets that satisfied grin on his face. What I don't understand is where he ever gets the time to think.

I know he does it a lot. I can tell because he writes what's really on his mind in his column in our paper and it's very thoughtful, reflective writing. Insightful ... there is the exact word.

Somehow he finds time to take the long view, to look into his own heart and those of all the people around him. He doesn't lecture, doesn't preach, but he watches life around him closely, and manages to find common ground. He finds things we all share rather than things to separate us. He finds the most amazing stuff right here in our back yard ... courage ... hope ... freedom ... dreams ... you will find all that here dear reader. I hope it serves you well.

Thanks,
David Crosby

Editor's note

Faster and next are two words that define our culture. Familiarity, on the other hand, is a comfort we seldom realize anymore and we are poorer for it.

Today's technology is tomorrow's relic, nearly in real time. Public conversation is often limited to catch-phrases such as "how're you doing", "have a nice day" or "good to see you."

The essays in this collection are as familiar as old friends. Here you will discover and rediscover the moments in life that cause joyous recognition.

Here you will recognize yourself recognizing yourself. Here you will find open doors and open windows. Here is a softness, a smoothness that begs to be touched.

Please come in, friend, and make yourself comfortable.

- Sterling Price

Introduction

This book picks up from where my last one left off, and like the last time, I did a lot of playing around with the sequence before deciding on "the final order."

My first inclination was to start this collection off with some of my latest writings because, as is often the case, I am most excited about what I'm writing *now* and what I'm writing *next*. I wanted people who might be reading it from front to back to get some of the recent stuff right at the beginning. At the same time, I knew that many people who read my last book didn't read it from front to back, they "opened it to any page," and let it speak to them in that way. With the power of synchronicity in mind, I went through a detailed process in an attempt to achieve a *meaningful random order*. In the end, I wound up favoring a chronological sequence as a reflection of my evolution.

"There is here with a T in front" covers the time period from February 1999 through October 2001. Though the columns are referenced by date, they are not, other than a few exceptions, about things that happened on or around that date or in any particular locale. They deal mainly with the self discovering itSelf, which is an event or a process that is uncontained in time.

- RC
11/01

Table of Contents

Out of the quantum world and into a perfectly clear confusion

About a hundred years ago, in a self-described "act of desperation," physicist Max Planck proposed quantum theory to account for some mysterious facts about light which could not be explained by the laws and equations of Sir Isaac Newton's "Classical" mechanics. Planck's theory, which suggested that energy does not exist over an infinitely divisible range but only in very discreet units, called *quanta*, gave rise to some new and paradoxical descriptions of matter and energy.

Some of those descriptions, such as the one that characterizes light as, simultaneously, *bundles* of energy and also as *waves* of energy are, or at least *were*, weird to the classically trained mind.

Armed with Planck's equations, a bunch of other physicists got together and developed a consistent set of physical laws to explain not only how light can be wave and particle at the same time but other paradoxes as well, such as why we can never say for sure where anything exists. Thus, the answer to the question – where you at, man - or, where's your head at? - is really speculative. The whole set of new laws, when put all together, formed the new quantum mechanics, which was better than the old classical mechanics because it explained and pertained more. Even though it was wrought with uncertainty and apparent contradictions, still, it was closer to the truth, and thus, we were forced to accept it.

But as significant, both scientifically and philosophically, as the new laws might be, they remain for the most part irrelevant because we don't see where they have all that much to do with our day-to-day lives. The good old truisms, ones like what goes up must come down, still seem to apply, and until they don't, until, say, water runs uphill, or something strange like that starts happening, then why bother with how weird our Physics says the world is.

Besides, we don't need Physics to tell us its weird out there. When we hear about someone getting killed out on the freeway by some drive-by shooter, or we see seemingly intelligent people choosing to be in abusive relationships over and over again, or we hear of countries dropping bombs on other countries and blowing up cities to keep the peace, then we know full well it's weird.

But even though the world's weird, and at times wild and wonderful, it is, nevertheless, still mostly "normal," mostly explicable, mostly not too out of the ordinary.

Speaking, recently, before a gathering of the American Association for the Advancement of Science, a physicist from the US Department of Energy's Los Alamos laboratory suggested that the reason for that normalcy is a process called "decoherence."

Now, before I even attempted to begin to understand what the heck the guy was talking about, I considered, first, the word *coherence*, which I think of as a state of clear-headedness, but which my dictionary defines as "a logical connection" and as "sticking or holding together." I figured, in the same way that *frost* is the opposite of *de-frost*, and *compression* is the opposite of *de-compression*, and *to materialize* is the opposite of *to de-materialize*, so must decoherence suggest the opposite of coherence, though I was careful to point out that he was not using the word *incoherence*. I saw that in each of the other words, the *de-* is used to mean "undo." Thus, I considered decoherence as the process of undoing coherence.

So, without fully grasping his words, I took it that what he was saying is that the process that undoes logical connection, and that un-sticks or pulls things apart, saves us from "all sorts of trouble," including things disappearing into thin air, and some things being dead and alive at the same time.

In describing the "sorts of trouble" that quantum mechanics might present, the physicist repeatedly used the word "chaotic." Chaos refers to a state of confusion or disorder, and as any of us who have ever sensed that our beliefs do not adequately or accurately describe the results in our lives know, chaos can pertain to what's going on inside or outside.

Our ticket out of the chaos, according to the speaker, is to dispense with logic and to not be attached (the "undoing" of the "sticking or holding together" part.) It's the same advice that has been doled out by yogis, gurus and shamans for eons.

I admit, I don't really get the gist of what the guy was talking about, but it does suggest to me that the really strange stuff is strange only from our old way of understanding the universe, and that since we've obviously not yet reached our final point of ultimate understanding, stranger stuff awaits us yet, in the next further elucidation of "the truth."

February 9, 1999

The whispered words of the wintry wind

Having been away for a couple weeks, she asked, as we spoke on the phone, if things were getting greener. I remembered, but only *after* she asked, that they were, for what has struck my attention lately, even more than how the trees and the grasses look, has been how the *air* looks. It's whiter and more indistinct. The sunlight is noticeably less direct, and the air currents far more capricious. I've found this face of nature to be comforting in a strangely uncomfortable way.

What peace I arrive at, and what encouragement I take with me, stems from the implication of time and from the seasons themselves. 'Tis the basis of hope, I say, to know, with a knowing born of experience, that spring, summer, fall and winter do naturally flow into and out of one another. The constant outward reminder of movement and variation, of rhythm and respiration, provides us ample reason and rationale for not getting too downcast when "clouds" gather, for not getting too "blown away" when the winds shift direction, and for not going overboard in celebration when the sun shines on our affairs.

And, then again, as I notice the mountains and the trees, the ground and the sky, looking so differently than they did yesterday and than they surely shall tomorrow, it reminds me that we, too, have our different faces and different aspects that we show to the world at different times, and the message it leaves me with is – that it's OK. It's OK. If something as big, and solid, and invariable as the earth can vary as it does from day to day, then surely we can put up with our own and each other's changes.

Thus, cognizance of change is the comfort I declared.

As for the uncomfortable-ness about it, part of it might have to do with the fact that except for slight variations there are no exceptions. Nature plays no favorites, nor takes pity none upon the fool. There is a natural order, and there are universal laws, and no matter how we might wish it otherwise, our "little heart's desires" cannot rearrange it. We cannot, for instance, make it stay summer, and neither will our roses remain ever in bloom. (We can, however, find warmth and light and the easy livin' in our hearts and minds, and we can learn to appreciate the beauty in all things.)

As there are laws that govern the motions of the planets, and earthly phenomena such as the transformation of the caterpillar into the butterfly, so too are there laws governing our growth and development. We cannot skirt our way around them. We cannot charm our way to enlightenment, nor fake our way to wisdom. It's like going to the dentist – we can, if we want to, claim that we brush and floss daily, but if we don't, the dentist won't be fooled, for our "condition" will be but the result of our daily practices.

And there is another, closer component to the uneasiness that I sense swirling around in the wary wind that whispers these thoughts and words to me. It has to do with what I can only describe as the very delicate balance of things.

It is a balance between the outward and the inward, between movement and stillness, between a center of gravity and a flight of fancy, between permanence and impermanence. The lesson I receive is that we must change, for change is the one constant of life, but that our changes, like the changes of heaven and earth, should rightly be based on enduring laws.

As I walked this morning, I looked and listened and barely caught a glimpse and heard a sound, as if from around the corner. It was the whispering wind, and although I could hear it, and evoke it clearly, over and over and over again, it took me the whole rest of the day to extract some meaning and write it down.

Dylan said, "the answer is Blowin' in the Wind," but it occurs to me that there is no "one" answer, rather a whole bunch of answers swirling around. They are all bits and pieces of the truth, and like Nature, the truth is ever changing. The changes, though, are based on that which endures and remains constant.

February 25, 1999

Creating new tools, new colors and new capacities

Hammer ... screwdriver ... pliers ... wrench ... All great tools, but not a one of them will do you much good if you've got a big old log that you're needing to cut through. Likewise, each of us are equipped with a whole bunch of great tools that work splendidly for some jobs but are pretty much useless in other cases.

For instance, you might have dandy deltoids, terrific triceps, bodacious biceps and impeccable pectorals, but none of these muscles will help you to raise the spirits of someone in sadness ... or to lift the mantle of doubt ... or to hold back a memory.

Neither shall your razor sharp mind enable you to cut to the core of compassionate love, or to pierce the realm of suffering, or penetrate the mystery of faith. Nor shall your kind heart provide you with the discipline necessary to control your thoughts, or to learn from your mistakes.

I am reminded of the color wheel. You have your primary colors — your red, blue and yellow, and when you combine them you make new "secondary" colors, which give us our greens and purples and oranges. Similarly, we have our thoughts, our feelings, and our movements, which I perceive to be analogous to the primary colors. Correspondingly, when we combine them, or get them working together, then we create new capacities which enable us to perform new tasks such as "weaving a seamless garment," or "spinning the wheel of fire," or "flying on the wings of perception."

The same principle applies to our senses, as far as enriching our experience of the world. If we were to rely solely on sight, then we would never know the sweet stimulation of fresh-cut grass or the charged salt air. If we were to depend primarily on olfaction then we would miss the joyous songs of birds in the morning or silence in the night. And even if we process what we hear, see and smell, the experience remains incomplete if we notice not the gentle kiss of the breeze upon our brow or the taste of trustworthiness.

By fusing and harmonizing our various dimensions, we enter new dimensions with new rules and new possibilities. By blending our senses and capacities together, we, in effect, create a new organ, an integrated instrument. It's the technique and the secret for creating new colors. Living colors to create a living work of art.

None of us, no matter how versatile we are, can handle all

the tasks that pop up around our homes with but a single tool. Likewise, neither can we meet all the challenges of living with the tools of just one dimension.

Endeavor to create new tools, new colors, new capacities.

March 25, 1999

Breaking the barrier;
In pursuit of the Three-Minute Mile

Every now and then, an event so significant happens that it serves to expand the boundaries of "the realm of possibility." The Wright Brothers' historic flight at Kitty Hawk was one such event, or Neil Armstrong's walk on the moon, or Dr. Christian Barnard's first successful heart transplant. Another huge, though generally much less recognized, "horizon-expanding" event occurred 45 years ago on this very date when Roger Bannister became the first human being on record to run a mile in less than four minutes.

What makes it so significant is that, whereas these other incredible achievements entailed some technological triumph, albeit put together with a strong vision and an indomitable spirit, Bannister's achievement represented the transcending of a *psychological* barrier.

In the early 1950s, the pursuit of the four-minute mile captured public attention the world over. Efforts to shatter the mark were a hot news item. The record of 4:01 had stood for a decade, and while many athletes and interested others thought that it could and would be done, there were also plenty of pundits, doctors and scientists who suggested that an actual physiological barrier existed which limited human performance. The human body, they said, was simply not made to run that fast that far.

Bannister dispelled that myth, and who knows how many others in the process. Three weeks after he *removed* the mysterious four-minute barrier, another runner came along and ran it even faster, and then, less than three weeks after that, the time was improved upon yet again. It was as if Bannister, through his accomplishment, gave everyone else *permission* to follow him "beyond the barrier." To me, it provides one of the most blatant examples of what can happen once we stop thinking and telling ourselves that *it can't* happen.

Today, we're running after another milestone, another new and improved time, a whole new era – in communication, co-operation, problem-solving, harmony and understanding.

We think – yeah, maybe we can get there, maybe it can be done, but we're not sure. We're not sure if it's physically possible given this world's natural tendency towards chaos and disorder. We're not sure that if we extend forth our hand in friendship that someone's not going to slap it. Or that if we look people squarely in the eyes that it might not make them uncomfortable, and who knows what someone's liable to do once they're put on the spot and made to feel uncomfortable.

To "break the barrier," and reach the new milestone, requires that we change, but some of us will only be willing to change once we are convinced of others' willingness to do likewise.

I often think about and call that new time, that new day with it's new way, "The Three-Minute Mile." In keeping track of our efforts, I see us continuing to shave tenths and hundreds of a second off our times, bringing us closer and closer to our aim, which is that elusive Three-Minute Mile.

There are those, though, who would tell us that the attainment of the Three-Minute Mile is a fantasy, pure and simple, just as the naysayers did once Bannister and the other runners of his time started setting their sights on the four minute mile. I say the real barrier, the true obstacle that prevents people's bodies, minds and spirits from working together in concert has much more to do with the mind and the heart of the individual than it does with any object quality or condition of the world.

As was the case with the milers of Bannister's time, our training, our preparation, and the shape we are in surely have a bearing on our outcome and achievement, but so too does our state of mind and our state of heart.

I compare our present reality to that decade when we were stuck on four minutes and one second. We break the barrier once we allow a world of enhanced communication and greater cooperation, a more harmonious world, to penetrate our consciousness and come into being within our own lives. For us, that's the equivalent of shattering the four-minute mile, and as we learned from the example of Bannister, once one person does it, it becomes easier for others to duplicate it. As more and more people start to allow the possibility of greater communication and greater understanding then we will notice greater and more hopeful changes in the world, and that will represent the Three-Minute Mile.

Still, I think some people have more fun sitting around analyzing and complaining about the old or the existing world than they do taking part in the creation of a new day and a new way. *They* represent the inertia of our present reality. Inertia is a close cousin to momentum, and knowing that provides us with a clue for how to overcome the inertia, which is but a tendency to resist change. According to a slogan that hangs on many lockerroom walls, enthusiasm creates momentum. Likewise, the way to overcome the inertia of our present reality, and to set about creating the new reality, is to enthusiastically undertake the conversion of humanity.

So strap on your running shoes, even you people with walkers and in wheel chairs, for the Three-Minute Mile is within our sights.

May 6, 1999

What to hold on to and what to put down

Everything was going along just fine. I had a delicious dinner going in the oven, and a plan for the rest of the night, but then, all of a sudden-like, things got decidedly un-fun.

I think the problem was that there were a couple of things I still *had* to do which, I knew, would likely be encroaching upon the things I still *wanted* to do.

Like the phone interview I had lined up to fill in the details on the story I was writing. It's not that I didn't feel like talking to the person, nor did I have any problem with writing the story, it was just a matter of the time, and a feeling that *my* time was being gobbled up.

Little things became big things, and *every*thing became a hassle, and the most graceful way out of the night seemed to lie in calm repose. Sleep held the promise of digestion; frustration-assimilation.

And when the morning light shot through the blinds and stirred me from my slumber, there came to me this image of a man carrying a cauldron. It was me, and the cauldron was full of water. And I had this feeling that I needed to pick up this other thing which was not as big as the cauldron, but which was rounded, and required at least one hand from me, but I couldn't remove one hand because I was holding on to the cauldron.

And the me that was laying there in bed laughed as I thought about the night before.

Sometimes it helps, or at least it helps me, to have models to guide my imagination, which, I'm pretty sure, is why I majored in physics.

It's almost like the tarot or the I Ching, where a single character or image corresponds to an expanded and detailed interpretation or commentary. For me, from now on, when I become aware that my preoccupation with something is keeping me from getting on with something else, there's a good chance I'll recall the image of the man with the cauldron, and I will remind myself that **sometimes you have to put something down before you can pick something else up.**

But sometimes, you just feel like holding on to it for a while, and you feel (like I felt), that your arms are plenty strong to hold on a while longer. And, no doubt, they are, but as the image implies, you make a choice as to what it is that you're going to carry around.

And as I got myself up and about, and as I moved around and the day moved on, I found myself remembering the Zen saying: "Chop wood, carry water," which I associate with "Be Here Now."

It's about not being distracted from one task by the thought of another task. In other words, you can't chop wood while you're carrying water, and you can't carry water while you're chopping wood. You do the one when it's time for the one, and the other when it's time for the other. Which is not to suggest that you can't walk and chew gum at the same time. It's a matter of recognizing when the one is distracting you from the other.

Maybe it's a case where the urge to communicate is what's blocking the communication. Where the desire to be understood is what's preventing the understanding. Sometimes, we want, so badly, for others to see and feel how hard our lives can be. Sometimes, that's the cauldron, and sometimes you have to set the cauldron down.

If and when you become aware of yourself "carrying the cauldron," then try and remember to remind yourself what "that other thing" is that you still have to pick up, for in that moment will the opportunity arise for you to conceive of something higher. Not only that, but to go ahead and put down the object, or suspend the behavior, or change the mind-set, that is keeping you tied to the lower.

Higher-lower, faster-slower, sounds like a judgment call to me. And that's what it is – learning to use our better judgment.

> *"The thing to do is to supply light and not heat."*
> —Woodrow Wilson

May 12, 1999

Doing the steps out on the steps – tapping into some memories

I first started stair-dancing back in the mid-1970s. Whenever I had a pretty good flight of stairs in my path, I'd sort-of-sideways of dance my way up or down.

I remember doing it my first day of college. It was on the campus of the University of Pennsylvania. I was on my way up to the football coach's office next to Franklin Field, and I danced my way on up the stairs. The track coach happened to be walking out of the building, and he spied me shuffling up the steps with a much bigger football-looking guy by my side, and he said, "You must be a db," as in defensive back, and he was right.

I guess I picked up the stair-dancing from watching those old Shirley Temple movies, where she and Bill "Bojangles" Robinson, would do their routines on the staircases of those Southern mansions. And while my routine was nothing like their routine, it was from their routine that my routine sprung forth.

"I knew a man Bojangles
and he danced for you
In worn out shoes,
With silver hair, a ragged shirt,
and baggy pants,
The old soft shoe."

Bill Robinson was orphaned at the age of six, so he started dancing for dough on the streets and in the beer gardens of Richmond, Virginia. Before too long, he hooked up with a traveling troupe and took his act on the road, and soon, he was hoofing it on vaudeville stages. He was a hit. So much so, that by

1908 he was knocking down $3,500 a week.

"He danced for those
at minstrel shows
and county fairs,
Throughout the South."

Robinson did this one lick that he called "the camel dance." It was rediscovered about 70 years later, and given the name "the moonwalk."

In the '30s and '40s, Robinson had an outstanding film career, including a role in the first all-black motion picture, "Harlem's Heaven," made in 1932.

In 1938, he bought a professional baseball team, along with James "Soldier Boy" Semler. The team was the New York Black Yankees. They lasted until 1948, the year after Jackie Robinson, no relation to Bill as far as I can tell, was signed by the Brooklyn Dodgers. After that, there was no more need for a black league.

Bill Robinson died a year later.

Though they called him "Bojangles," and though parts of the story sound somewhat the same, Bill Robinson is not the Mr. Bojangles popularized in the great Jerry Jeff Walker song which, according to him, is a true story.

"I met him in a cell
in New Orleans I was
Down and out ..."

"... He said 'I dance
now at ev'ry chance
in honky tonks,
For drinks and tips.

But most the time I spend
behind these county bars
'Cause I drinks a bit.'"

I suppose it was on account of the kind of character portrayed in Jerry Jeff's song, and the kind of servant roles that Bill Robinson played in those Shirley Temple films, that tap dancing kind of died out in the '50s, '60s and early '70s. To the "socially conscious" people of the time who were trying to feel and perpetuate pride, tap dancing was a reminder and a remnant of their slave days. And it was, for tap dancing originated with the black slaves who saw and imitated the Irish jigs, the Virginia reels and the Lancashire clogging, only they infused it with their own African sense of rhythm.

Today, tap is alive and well, thanks to hoofers like Gregory Hines and Savion Glover.

I remember an interview I saw one time with Gregory Hines where he was talking about the much younger Savion, who burst on to the scene in the mid-'80s. Hines said, though not word for word, "It wasn't until I was in my late 30s that I could truly express myself through tap dancing. I'm talking about getting an idea, and expressing it in the moment that it occurs to you. Savion could do that when he was 12 years old."

To me, what made that comment even more awe-inspiring was that Hines was the one who said it.

The Sufis have a saying that goes something like: "More meaningful is the praise of one master than of 1,000 amateurs."

As for tap, Savion calls it, "My means of expression. When I'm feeling down or depressed, I literally dance that feeling away."

It's similar to the way some of the great old blues singers talk about the music – as a tool to help them feel better. And while the description might sound like the blues, the foundation and development of tap is more closely associated with jazz.

Speaking, one time, about the secret to his expression and achievement, jazz great Miles Davis said, "It's because I don't remember anything."

The art of forgetting, of not being tethered to the past, and not clinging to static form or to an unchanging set of rules may indeed be a key to greatness when it comes to creative expression. But it is in remembering – remembering people like Bill "Bojangles" Robinson that the greatness of that expression lives on.

"Mr. Bojangles,
Mr. Bojangles,
Mr. Bojangles,
Dance."

May 24, 1999

Don't drop the potato

I have a friend who took a trip recently to New Orleans so that he could get his fill of some good live music. For a few weeks after he got back, he was often heard saying, "Let the good times roll," which is a popular slogan and attitude towards life in the Crescent City.

"*Laissez le bon temps rouler,*" say the town's French-speaking inhabitants.

I met another guy, 10 or so years ago, who shared with me a less well known slogan that has meaning and is whispered among the Acadians of the bayou region.

"Don't drop the potato," the man murmured.

To understand what it means, it helps to know a bit about the Acadians.

Acadia was a French colony in eastern Canada, consisting of the present Maritime Provinces. The St. Lawrence River was one of the most important waterways in the European settlement of North America, and since Acadia, or *Acadie,* as the French called it, was located at the mouth of the St. Lawrence River, the French and the British were constantly fighting over control of the place. The Acadians, those French-speaking inhabitants who were already well settled in to the area, and who lived in peace with the friendly Micmac Indians, didn't take part in the fighting.

In 1621, James I of England granted Acadia to England, and re-named it Nova Scotia. After the King's decree, the British, who were firmly in control of the place at the time, started getting fearful that there might be an uprising among the Acadians and the Micmac. So they gave everyone an option – either pledge an oath to England, or split. The Acadians, like the Micmac, derived their identity, their sense of who they were, from their customs and their language, and they weren't about to abandon that, so they were deported, and scattered all along the East Coast of the continent.

In his great poem "Evangeline," Longfellow told the story of two lovers, Evangeline and Gabriel, who were separated during the deportation of the Acadians. They lived in the village of Grand Pre. One night, the English came and took away all the men from the village, made them prisoners, and then shipped them off. The next night, the British returned and burned everything in the village. Evangeline was exiled, and she spent the rest of her life walking around looking for her true love. She became a Sister of Mercy, and in a Philadelphia shelter for poor people, she found Gabriel as he was dying.

To the Acadians, or the Cajuns as they're called down in Louisiana, Evangeline represents all Acadians, and Gabriel represents their home, with the hope being that, like the lovers in the story, they will one day again be reunited.

Which brings us to the potato. It's a hot potato, which means it's hard to hold on to.

"The potato," explained my mysterious friend, "is the dream of finding our love and returning home. It's the dream of a better life, and you gotta hold on to it. You can't let go of it. Even when things are bad, and life gets grim, don't drop the potato."

There are a whole slew of sayings that we can use like mantras to help us keep our strength and courage up, and our hope alive.

In their anthem, "Stand Up For Your Rights," Bob Marley and Peter Tosh sing and keep repeating, *"Don't give up the fight."* Sailors struggling at sea shout, "Don't give up the ship!" I'll relay the message of the Acadian who said, "Don't drop the potato," and I'll say it in this way:

Hot times might make you sweat
And wish that you could just forget
All your sorrow and all your pain
But all your suffering has not been in vain
So when the bad news comes along
Don't forget this freedom song,
[It goes:]
Rise up, oh rise above
Fly away on the wings of your love
Hold on, baby, don't let go
And don't you drop the potato.

May 27, 1999

Zone therapy;
new rays call for new ways

I found it interesting that the subject of the first e-mail I received this morning was: "Cards win as ozone hole repairs itself," because last night, in the middle of the night, I awoke from a deep sleep, grabbed the pen and the pad that I leave on the nightstand beside my bed, and jotted down a note to myself that had to do, specifically, with the ozone layer. As it turned out, the e-mail letter didn't have *anything* to do with the ozone, it was just the sender's sense of humor, but I found the mention of it significant nonetheless.

Now, even though I'm a sensitive guy, it's not like I regularly stir from my slumber because I'm distressed over some environmental abuse or another. There's usually some other more personal reason for my tossing and turning, and in this case, what did wrest me from my rest was a burn across my chest ... and stomach, and shoulders, and arms. A sunburn. One of the wicked sort. Cardinal red. Crimson tide. Ruby Tuesday. A real beet poet.

Talk about taking me by surprise — we were just sitting out on the porch talking, and for not more than a couple hours at most. Granted, I had my shirt off, but heck, I, with my olive skin, used to be able to stay out all day and not get nearly as scorched as I did this time. I knew right away that it was the result of a decimated ozone layer, but I didn't comment on it until the middle of the night, when I awoke suddenly, flicked on the light and wrote: "Perhaps in no other area is it more apparent to me that the world has changed - that things aren't the way they used to be - than in the area of sunbathing-suntanning-sunburning."

It's a different sun than it used to be, with much more dangerous rays. You can't treat them the same as the old ones. New rules apply.

It's like the situation out on the freeways. In the old days, when someone cut you off or boxed you in or followed a little too closely, a shake of the head or some other look of disgust to let the person know what you thought of his driving, was not all that risky of a response. But nowadays, you can't be sure that such a look won't send someone over the edge and onto the warpath. You have to really beware which, as my friend Paul Williams pointed out, means *Be aware.*

And it's good advice, too, when it comes to deciding how

you're gonna hang out in the sun.

Nowadays, that's an industry unto itself, and our pharmacy shelves are filled with an array of products made to block out the sun – all these creams with numbers on the bottles which indicate how effectively they shield you from the rays. Me, I usually still rely on hats and bandanas, and other clothing, and on the clock, to help ease me in to summertime levels of exposure, because I just don't like the feeling or the thought of creams clogging up my pores. But I do, nevertheless, realize how necessary it is, especially for the fair-skinned folk among us. And so I put forth this reminder – not only to be careful in the sun, but to know also that each time we spray an aerosol can, or use a styrofoam cup, or an inorganic fertilizer, we deliver another blow and swipe another slash into the protective layer around our planet.

And you can be hard-headed, or closed-minded, and not acknowledge the changes that have taken place, and not adapt your behavior accordingly, but it's your own hide that's gonna get fried. Reported occurrences of skin cancers and other ailments, and of medical procedures, having to do with exposure to the sun, are at an all-time high. Sun-block is one thing, but we need to develop some other kind of defense against the sun. Our evolution calls for it.

I suggest that we learn to create a sort of polarized lens in our minds. That is, a filter, a doorway that will only allow to pass through its portal those things, waves, vibrations that are going in a certain direction. It's like if you want to move your bed into the next room, you have to tilt it in order for it to fit through the door. In the case of the psychic "filter," we only let in those vibrations and effects that are in the direction of healing ... protection ... provision.

I've been doing the same thing with food lately, by intending to take on and assimilate the nutritional, medicinal and sensual value of the food, while denying, rounding up, and incinerating all of the unhealthy aspects and using the resultant flame as fuel to benefit the world in some other way.

We're talking about the ozone layer. The symbol for the ozone molecule is O3; O – O – O. So while we are building our polarized lens, we can also endeavor to replenish the ozone by personally becoming O3. Say, for instance, going **Organic**, which would eliminate harmful chemicals that destroy our outer cover, and becoming more **Open**-minded and **Open**-hearted.

In the meantime, I think I'll continue to wear a t-shirt to cover myself... at least, until I resume my sit-ups and aerobics routine.

June 2, 1999

Let's get a few things straightened out here; relaxation through organization

... Like trying to put 10 gallons of paint into a five gallon can ...

... It's sure to leave a mess.

Such is the situation in our home. Just too much stuff in too small a space. So there's always things "out," lying around.

Granted, most of it is due to our "ah, let it go for now" attitude, but some of it is definitely a function of "volumetrics." Again, too much stuff in too little a space.

The Zen answer is simple – get rid of some of the stuff.

I know so many people who have consciously lightened their loads in the past few years by getting rid of stuff, and who seem so much lighter and more relaxed as a result of it. Makes sense. Think about how many psychological studies have been done that describe the effects of overcrowding. How it can make you crazy. Normally, they're talking about urban plight, city life. Crowded streets and crowded sidewalks. Noise and hostility. People living and working above and below you, in front of and behind you, to the right and to the left. And everywhere you turn, you have to deal with someone else, and their stuff. But it applies, too, to your own stuff and to your own space.

I'm constantly trying to "thin out" the home environment, because the more the stuff piles up the more it "chokes" me off. 'Course, we live in a culture that promotes and perpetuates a predisposition to accumulate stuff, and here I think of those bumper stickers that read: "He who dies with the most toys wins."

I don't buy into that, not even a little bit. It's like John Lennon said – *"You can't take nothing with you but your soul."*

As for soul, when I look into the mirror of mine, I am forced to admit that I'm not the neatest, most tidy person around. But I'm working on it.

The study of Physics teaches us that the world naturally and automatically tends towards disorder. Gurdjieff teaches us that a "conscious act" is the opposite of an automatic tendency. Thus, a conscious environment is an ordered environment. And what could be more ordered than emptiness? Which is why I want my space to be emptier.

In physics, we call empty space a "vacuum." It is a space that contains nothing. At this point, the perfect vacuum is purely a theoretical matter, for as far as we know, there is no place, no space, that contains "nothing."

It occurs to me that that's the goal of meditation – to become a vacuum, to contain "nothing," to know the Void.

Part of the problem, for me, is not knowing when and how to get rid of things. For instance, I had this huge, old, outdated computer jammed into the corner of a closet that was bulging with stuff and had become a huge hassle to get in and out of. I'd wanted to get rid of it for a long time. I offered it to the school, but they didn't want it. It seemed futile and otherwise bothersome to try and sell it for a few measly bucks, and I couldn't think of anyone to give it to who might have any use for it, yet, it didn't seem right to just throw it out either. The part of me that knows about Japan making a bunch of money by selling off its garbage knows that the real waste is to waste an opportunity. It seemed like I should get *something* for this thing that had cost me more than a thousand dollars. But then one day, I realized I was *still* paying for it, not with money, but with time and energy. With the minutes that I spent looking for things that I knew were in that closet but had a hard time finding. And when I finally got to that point, I hurled the whole system into an empty dumpster, and I felt like one of those rock stars you hear about who throw things out hotel windows.

As another example of not knowing the when and the how of lightening the load, take all those old bills and receipts, records, letters and business correspondences. We're taught to hold on to them for our own protection, in case something should pop up and bite us from behind. But as you fill up another basket, another envelope, another file, another folder, another drawer, another cabinet, another box and another closet, all the things that are supposed to be there for your protection and convenience start becoming the source of your anxiety, for there is no solace in clutter.

It's like - when I walk around with empty pockets, I don't pay it any attention. I don't sit there patting at my pockets, wondering what's where. But if I should drop just a couple of items in, say my knife, my keys or a couple of coins, then I'm constantly checking, taking stock of my holdings.

Bearing in mind the time I waste and the amount of distress I cause myself looking for things that I know I have but I don't know where, I resolved to turn this time into Cleanup Time, and I immediately started singing the chorus to the John Lennon song of the same name.

However, far we travel,
Wherever we may roam,
The center of the circle,
Will always be our home,
No friends and yet no enemies,
Absolutely free,
No rats aboard the magic ship,
Of (perfect) harmony,
Now it begins,
Let it begin
Cleanup Time,

June 7, 1999

Wishing on a star and a flower

"Star light, Star bright.
First star I see tonight,
Wish I may, wish I might,
Have the wish I wish tonight."

I've found myself reciting this child's poem the last two nights, at the precise moment that I notice and become entranced by the bright star in the west, reaching me from about "seven-shades-of-blue up" from the night-time but not yet fully dark-time horizon. It seemed the only star in the sky, as it wrenched the words from my heart. And as I heard myself saying them I thought, well, if I'm going to petition this star to make my wish come true then I darn well better get my wish together in my mind.

Elizabeth Barrett Browning wrote: *"Every wish is like a prayer with God,"* and since it was God I was talking to anyhow and not just some condensed ball of hydrogen, I went ahead and prayed, earnest and true. I didn't have any words to wrap my prayer in, but as the 17th Century English preacher, John Bunyan, said: *"In prayer, it is better to have heart without words, than words without a heart."*

Bunyan wrote "The Pilgrim's Progress," which chronicles the journey of the hero, who in this case, is called "Christian." Christian moves from the City of Destruction, through the Slough of Despond, over the Hill of Difficulty, through the Valley of Humiliation, and on into the terrifying Valley of the Shadow of Death. He passes through Vanity Fair, is held captive by Giant Despair in Doubting Castle, and after crossing the bridgeless River of Death, arrives and is received in the Celestial City.

Some say it's an accurate allegory for the journey of the soul.

As for the captivating star in the sky, I figured, considering how big and bright it was that it probably wasn't a star at all, but rather, a planet. And since all our planets are named after Roman gods, who are but Greek gods with the names changed, except for Pluto and Uranus, I wondered which god it was that I was bouncing the prayer off of. That is, which planet it is that shines so prominent in the western sky at this time of year, at this time of night.

I can usually manage to find such information pretty quickly, but for some reason, on this particular night, I was having a bit more difficulty.

After letting me flounder around through books and on the web for a while, my lady said, "I bet my sister knows."

Her sister, after all, was a counselor, many moons ago, at The Campfire Girl summer camp, and she taught my gal what in the sky is where and when, and since my gal knows more about such things than I do, I went ahead and phoned her sister.

"I think it's Jupiter," she said, on the other end of the line. "If you have some binoculars you can tell for sure by the moons. Even with a simple pair of field glasses you should be able to see at least one if not two of the moons."

I don't have any binoculars, so I looked through my camera, but I couldn't tell that way. I then blurred my vision and looked sideways, and I'm pretty sure I saw one of the moons sitting just beneath the light of the planet, and I said, "... Jupiter, ha? "

It's the name the Romans gave to the Greek god Zeus, who was the first and most powerful of all the gods that rule mankind.

Zeus was the son of Cronus and Rhea, who were both brother and sister and man and wife. They were the children of Uranus (the sky) and Gaea (the earth.)

It reminds me of the John Lennon song, "Yer Blues," where he sings:

"*My father was of the sky, My mother was of the earth, I am of the Universe, and you know what that's worth.*"

Did Lennon have Zeus as the singer of the song, or was he comparing himself to the greatest of all Greek gods? And why shouldn't he, for does it not say, "*I AM* the Lord thy God," not "*HE IS* the Lord thy God?" And also, "Ye shall have no other gods before *Me*," not "Ye shall have no other gods before *Him*."

And as I was pondering it, the phone rang. I figured it was probably the sister calling me back to tell me for sure which planet it was in the sky, but it wasn't her voice, which caught me off guard. It was her friend, calling to say, "You know that star … well, she thinks it's Jupiter, but I say it's Flora," which is the name we've given to, and which was claimed by, our eight-month-old daughter. Eight months, that is, if you count from the time of conception and not from the time of birth, which is one way of saying she's due next month.

And I smiled to think that the star is a planet, and that the planet is a flower, and that she shines upon our lives from what Longfellow called "the infinite meadow of heaven."

Oh, twinkle, twinkle little star
How I wonder where you are
Like I often think about
The flower who has yet to sprout
And how life will change,
And how it will be,
When two who are one become three

"In eastern lands they talk in flowers, and tell in a garland their loves and cares."

- James Gates Percival

June, 1999

Time, like space, is of no use if we get not wiser

I heard, today, that according to the latest US Census report, the median age in the United States is now 36 years old, which means that there are an equal number of people who are older than 36, as there are younger than 36. At first, you might not know what to make of that, but consider that that is the *oldest median age ever* on record for this country.

... The oldest median age. It means more people are alive at an older age than ever before.

The more people part of that statement is on account of the baby boom. You look back over the birth statistics, and you see that there was a sharp increase in the number of people born in the United States beginning in 1946, and the number of births remained "high" until about 1964, and then it tapered off. Nowadays, the number of children born in a year is about the same as it was in the mid-1950s, but the population is much greater, so the birth *rate* is actually down.

The *older* part of the statement comes from the advancements we've made; specifically, the advances in technology and medicine. We're getting better at both ends of the spectrum. Less people are dying in infancy or early childhood, and more people are living longer.

In 1920, for instance, the average life expectancy for a person in the U.S, including both sexes and all races, was 54 years old. By 1950, it had increased to 68 years old. In 1998, it's 78. A 24-year increase in our expected life span in just 78 years. That means that about every three years, we gain another year of living. I'm 40 now, so even if things *only* continue at the present rate of advance, when I'm 43 my life expectancy will then be listed at 79. At 46 it will have increased to 80. At 49 – 81; 52 – 82; 55 – 83; 58 – 84; 61 – 85; 64 – 86; 67 – 87; 70 – 88; 73 – 89; 76 – 90; 79 – 91; 82 – 92; 85 – 93; 88 – 94; 91 – 95; 94- 96; 97 – 97.

Ninety-seven. That's what my *adjusted* life expectancy is right now if things continue at the present rate. If our advancement accelerates at all, which you know it will, then I should live to be even older than that.

Median means "right in the middle," which is one way of measuring "the average." Thus, it is justified to say that for the average person today, 50 years old is the beginning of "middle age."

A few things occur to me about this living longer and this delayed entry into middle age. The first thing is that it creates a greater need and a greater opportunity for us to learn how to appreciate life. If, for instance, you find life to be a drag, then it's going to be drag for a longer amount of time, and that doesn't sound like much fun, nor does it seem that that would serve or benefit others. If, on the other hand, you "groove" on life, then, likewise, you get to groove for even longer, and what could be better, I ask, than grooving?

"I can't imagine anything that's better,
The world is ours whenever we're together,
There ain't a place I'd like to be instead of
Groovin."

— Felix Cavaliere / Eddie Brigati

To me, groovin' means being alive, aware, relaxed and in the moment. If we plan on making the years count, rather than just sitting around counting the years, then we best learn how to groove.

Another thing about living longer is that you have to provide for yourself, or be provided for, materially-speaking, for a longer period of time. Either that, or we as a society or us as individuals have to evolve beyond materialism. *I think that can happen.* Then again, I heard something about the International Space Station today, and it had me recalling my first real involvement, more than 20 years ago, with the issue of living and working in space. Back then, I studied many facets of colonization, and thought it to be a wonderful solution to some of our biggest problems, including, energy shortages, overpopulation, jobs, the environment, and the threat of nuclear war. But in order for it to become a great solution, it requires that we become a *wiser* people. And when I think of all the wars and hate crimes and environmental disregard that still go on today I think, what good is a space colony if it's just a place for us to bring our wretchedness and unawareness.

As for middle age, and people being younger older, it's a way of saying, "It's OK, you still got time," while at the same time, emphasizing that there's not much time left for wasting.

Having more time to gain experience is like having a few lifetimes in one to learn what life on earth has to teach us.

This presupposes that the earth will even still be here for us to grow old.

In any case, regardless of how old we might eventually grow to be, unless we tune into the Ageless Wisdom, unless we continue to "die" to all the earthly attachments so that we can be "born" unto the Spirit, unless we transcend the cycle of birth and death, then living shall remain short-lived, and an illusion.

June 16, 1999

Seek out and find a broader experience

"I know this road like the back of my hand. I can drive it in my sleep." The problem is that when it becomes so familiar, we often do fall asleep on the road. I'm not talking about the road that leads from this town to that town; I'm talking about the road we travel through life.

Whenever something becomes routine it no longer demands our attention. That's why the police and firefighters train for "situations," so that if they find themselves entering into one of those situations, life and death situations, then their training and their instincts, which are faster than their decision-making process, can take over and direct them to the appropriate response. It's why musicians practice scales for hours on end – so that they become proficient at playing their instrument without having to think about it. And when they don't have to think about it, then they can get to a place that is beyond thought, where they can express themselves in the present. It's why athletes work on the fundamentals over and over, so that the execution becomes automatic. If they can remain "above" the distractions, then the Self can take over.

But, like any of the coins jiggling around in your pocket, repetition has two sides. And the other side of being "present" is being "absent."

Take your day, for instance. Maybe you've got a morning routine to start things out, and you know exactly how long it takes you to get ready for work. And you go through that routine in the same way, in pretty much the same order, and you don't have to think about it. And since you don't have to think about it, sometimes you just don't think at all. And what sometimes happens is, you arrive at work having not thought about things. And once you're at work you have to think about work-things, that is, if you have to think at all. And if the job should become mere repetition, to the point where you hardly even have to think about it, then another whole chunk of your day is spent in a kind of thoughtlessness. And then there's the time you spend with the one, or the ones, you're traveling through life with. The time at home. Is it predictable according to the TV guide, and by what night of the week it is; by the hour or the half-hour? And do you talk about things that are on your mind ... that are from your heart?

Do you make decisions about things, and I don't mean decisions on whether to buy something or not. If not, and if the days are the same, the standardized stereotypical same, then you probably could have learned just as much and experienced just as much by never even having woken up in the first place; by just staying in bed and going back to sleep. Which, in a sense, is what you've done if you were absent throughout the day.

In preparing for this baby, I've read and heard that the best thing you can do for your child, besides just loving her, is to provide the broadest possible sensory experience you can. To stimulate the senses, all the senses, as much as possible because it gets those neurons firing, which in turn activates the brain. I would say it's a good prescription, too, for adults, for we could all certainly use a few tricks, or techniques, to help kindle our interest, arouse our passion, provoke our awareness, and elicit our attention.

And while we are inundated with a barrage of sensory information all the time, much of it is like the white noise on the radio. It's static, and we tune it out.

I got to thinking along these lines today as I was driving through the neighborhood on a road I don't normally travel. It struck me that not much has really struck me lately, and I knew that it was just a matter of paying attention. For how, I asked myself, could one not be struck when there is so much beauty, and pain, and mystery, and folly in the world? It's like Croz said the other day, "You can't walk more than 50 feet down any block in this country and not find something."

The thing is, when the scenery is the same from day to day, then there's a tendency to not look as closely, to not see it anew. It becomes part of the pattern, like the wallpaper.

But it's not always possible, and perhaps, neither is it preferable to travel a different route, which bespeaks the involvement and the importance of our inner faculties when it comes to "quality of experience."

As far as the bit about the broadest possible sensory experience, it applies as much, if not more, to the inner as to the outer.

If we could learn to self-activate our senses then we would have the capacity to always bring the world alive. It's an acquired talent, which takes a lot of practice with all the senses.

I know a lot of people who use visualization, which, no doubt, is a potent tool and a valuable technique. But if our inner progress is skewed towards the visual, then we might not develop the capacity to "hear" our heart talking, or "feel" what our spirit is urging, or "smell" an opportunity, or "taste" the true bitterness and sweetness of life's disappointments and triumphs.

The challenge is to continually seek and find ways to broaden and freshen our experience. It could be something as simple as trying out a new kind of food, or taking a different route home, or turning off the television. Or it might require a bit more inner effort than that.

But the more we stimulate the senses, the more we activate the brain, which in turn, "initiates" new mental processes.

Many people have pondered the "mind-body connection," and they have asked the question "*where* is the mind *located?*" A better question would be *how* is the mind *used*, for it is through the use of the mind that we connect our brain to our heart and soul.

June 23, 1999

Evolving in the direction of freedom

"You tell me that it's e-vol-ution.
Well, you know, we all want to change ..."
　　- John Lennon

I remember, as a kid, learning about dinosaurs. I remember the plastic figurines, and the spectacular illustrations, and I remember and still know the difference between a brontosaurus, a stegosaurus and a tyrannosaurus rex. And I remember the questions and even some of the answers pertaining to why the dinosaurs became extinct, such as brain size and geological phenomena. That's why I took interest the other day when I heard the paleontologist say: *"Not all of the dinosaurs disappeared."* Some of them evolved into other things, like birds. And once they started flying, then they started changing in other ways, such as becoming a whole lot smaller, so as to become *better* flyers.

[Which brought to mind the moments I've had where I think I remember going through the transition period from water to land. Where I can feel myself floating just beneath the surface, seeing others who have already made it out, as well as the remnants of the many who tried but were not prepared to live on the outside.

And I have remembered, too, breaking the surface, and moving out and making the land my home, and making it through the shift.

And I have often felt that I am and we are again on the brink and at the threshold, approaching a time when we move into a new world with a new set of circumstances.

In other words, I have sensed our evolution. I've had a conversation with a whale regarding it, and when I stood alone at night in the Sonora desert, and saw the mysterious lights, I felt like I was seeing myself in the future. It suggests a continuity of all life and all consciousness existing as an evolutionary progression.]

And it occurred to me that birds, since they can move through the three dimensions of right-left, front-back and up-down, represent a greater state of freedom than dinosaurs and the two dimensions they move in, and I thought — suppose the dinosaurs *didn't* become extinct, suppose they just got freer. I regarded evolution not in some *random* fashion, but as having a direction. And that that direction – which I call Godward – is in the direction of freedom.

The question may arise that if being able to move up and down as well as back and forth and right and left represents a state of greater freedom, then why haven't we, who have much bigger brains than dinosaurs, all sprouted wings and learned how to fly? Perhaps it is because we know and, like Dylan in his "Ballad in Plain D," ask: *"Are the birds free from the chains of the skyway?"*

We are aware of the reality, and yet, realize the limitation of a freedom based on physical characteristics, such as bigger, faster, stronger. We have, instead, developed mental capabilities that enable us to fly as high as the birds and beyond, and to plunge the depths of the ocean, and to move across the plains and prairies faster than the fastest of all four-legged creatures.

But despite all our magnificent achievements, we are still bound by our woes and worries, by our judgments and predispositions. The paradox is that the very thing that makes us freer, namely, the self-conscious mind, is the same thing that also hinders our freedom, for while the mind can open many of the "doors" to our evolution, it also puts up many of the barriers. In some cases, the only way to penetrate the barriers of the mind is through the action of the heart.

It's like the opera singer who breaks the glass by sustaining a single note at a certain pitch. If we could sing with our hearts, and hold on to a note that vibrates at the frequency of love, then we could shatter the container of hate. Likewise I can think of cases when courage (which is of the heart) is needed in order to overcome fear (which is of the mind.) Or when trust – in ourselves, in God, in the Universe – dispels the mistrust that has kept us from adventure, from rich interactions, and from a full and satisfying experience of life. In each case cited, the action of the heart overcomes the barriers of the mind.

And while I believe that the "opening of the heart" is a crucial mutation that must occur at this stage of our evolutionary journey, it's clear that not every impulse and movement of the heart is towards freedom. In some instances, true, we need heart action in order to overcome mind interference, but in others, we need the mind's discretion to regulate the heart's impetuosity. As for which one wins out in which situation, it is a matter of evolution.

Keep in mind that when I speak of evolution, I don't mean Evolutionism. I consider it evolution when a person, or a culture or a species gets wiser, or becomes more intelligent. And the wiser and the more intelligent we get, the freer we shall become.

The new traits to be evolved are not necessarily morphological features, but rather, mental, emotional, psychic and spiritual capacities and capabilities to make us freer.

Patrick Henry said: *"Give me liberty or give me death."* Michael on Fire said: *"Evolve or die."* If we consider freedom as the direction of our evolution, then it means the same thing.

June 30, 1999

Become whole –
join the integration generation

I heard a story on the national news about a woman who had been diagnosed with breast cancer, and who had chosen to treat it with a combination of chemotherapy and other, more "alternative" therapies, including massage, acupuncture and meditation. The point of the story was that the combination of conventional and "unconventional" healing methods, which they call the "integrative approach," really is better, and promotes greater recuperation, than either of the methods by themselves. And while it occurred to me that this could very well be a case of the "conventional" forces making use of the old "if you can't beat 'em, join 'em" strategy I agree that, for us at this time, integration is a critical concept and course of action.

To integrate means "to make whole by adding together or bringing together all the various parts." If something is *not* whole then it is partial, fragmented, incomplete.

In the case of our development as human beings, there is, at least, a physical, mental and emotional component to it. If a person were to develop in one of these realms while lagging far behind in another area, then not only would that person be unbalanced, but also *less than all* that he or she could be. In other words, partial, fragmented, not whole. The integrative approach would be to pay attention to and unify all of the various aspects that make us what we are and what we can be.

And there are aspects within aspects, which also call for integration.

For instance, in the case of our physical growth, our optimum development requires that we eat a nutritious diet, that we exercise, and that we get enough sleep. To severely lack in any of these areas would leave us unhealthy. And if we break each of these aspects down even further, we still see the value and necessity of the integrative approach.

Consider, for example, our diet. We can analyze and evaluate it in a number of different ways. We might count calories. We might focus on the macro-nutrients of protein, fats and carbohydrates. We might pay attention to the basic food "groups." Or we might even consider it from the perspective of yin and yang. But it's when we put them all together, in other words, integrate them, that we get the most complete picture of dietary health.

It's the same with exercise. Some people concentrate on strength training, some on cardiovascular, and others on flexibility. But a workout program that centers on one or even two of these areas is not as effective as a workout that incorporates all three. This, again, is an example of the integrative approach, this time in the area of physical fitness.

To use the integrative approach within our own lives is to pay proper attention to the physical, mental, emotional, intuitional, volitional, and whatever other aspects of ourselves and our functioning we can conceive of.

But if we are to fully utilize the integrative approach, then it doesn't end there. The task is not only to integrate ourselves, but to integrate the universe.

Our physics (and for some of us, our philosophy) teaches us that all things in the universe are interrelated and are, thus, part of a unified whole.

To the minds of us mortals evolving through the realms of time and space, the world may sometimes present problems and situations which would seem to indicate discord and lack of unity. But if we continually strive to achieve a view and an awareness that incorporates the disparate elements into a single unified whole, and that frames the plurality of creation into a picture of divine oneness, then likely are we to gain a greater understanding of it all. If we can detect unity through all the creative diversity then might we better be able to perceive a grand purpose without, and feel purpose within.

August 9, 1999

Food for thought, food for evolution

I've often made mention of how for my family and all of our Italian relatives, the kitchen was the center of the universe, and generally, all social interaction centered around food.

Well, if a recent report out of Harvard University of Minnesota is correct, then the supreme importance of food and cooking is not only limited to the Italian households, but is one of the most important factors directing our human evolution.

According to anthropologists from these two fine institutions, "The process of human evolution has to do with food and how it was prepared."

They note that before Homo erectus appeared, that is, our ancestors who started standing upright and walking around on two legs, that people (who really weren't quite people yet) had huge teeth suitable for chewing all day long, and that the males were much larger than females. But 1.9 million years ago, things changed. Teeth got much smaller, and both sexes got much bigger, though females increased in size a lot more than males, which effectively narrowed the size gap.

The reason for these changes, say the researchers, is because humans learned to build fires and cook. And specifically, to cook *roots.* The cooking softened the roots which, up to that point in time, they had been eating raw, and it made the nutrients in the roots more readily available. The softness meant that teeth didn't have to be so huge, and the more readily available nutrients meant that the people grew bigger.

But the physical changes weren't the only dramatic result of the cooking. It also changed the whole ritual of eating and, get this, mating.

Let's start with the eating part. Before fire, people just picked a root and ate it wherever they were, but once they started cooking, then they had to bring the food *back* to the place where they cook it. Cooking *then* was done in a common kitchen where other people, including larger and more dominant beings, could see the food... which opened the door to theft. So people had to learn to cooperate in other ways if they didn't want their own food ripped off. That is, people started watching out for each other. And since females were the most vulnerable to theft, it forced them to form bonds with males, in particular, males who would be willing to *cooperate* in defending the food supply.

As far as the mating part goes, it relates to the size issue. When the males were much larger than the females, mating was more of a harem system as is seen in among the gorillas. But, as the researchers pointed out, "when male and female mammals are close in size, pair-bonding is the rule."

Since eating cooked food made people bigger and stronger, which, from a an evolutionary standpoint is advantageous, people then tended towards pair-bonding and a sort of family unit around a hearth.

Another offshoot of cooking is that many of the roots that would have otherwise been poisonous if eaten raw, became a regular part of people's diets. So, people got a much greater *variety* in their diet.

If all this stuff is true, then the cooking is responsible, not only for changes in our physical structure, but also for making us more cooperative, more monogamous, and for introducing more variety into our everyday lives.

Again, the researchers point out that it's not only the cooking that was so important to our evolution, but specifically, the cooking of the *roots.*

I, too, have long felt that our evolution is dependent on the kind of food we eat. And here I speak not so much about the physical body, but about the other higher "bodies" that make up the whole of who and what we are.

Take the astral body, for instance. Clearly, it is less dense in it's makeup than the physical body, and so if we are hoping for growth in the astral body then naturally we require some kind of "finer," less dense food in our diet. Likewise, the mental body, the spiritual body and the angelic body all exist at correspondingly higher and higher vibratory rates, and in order for them to develop, they require a greater supply of finer and finer foods. Light and sound and fragrance come immediately to mind. These are the new foods driving our evolution at present.

I am reminded of the saying: *"You are what you eat,"* and so, I shall strive continually to keep always on my plate a main course of "love," along with a side serving of "patience," "understanding," "courage" and "compassion," and season it all with a sparkling of "humor."

August 12, 1999

Maxim 8.14: Babies are like golf

Some of my friends and neighbors have mentioned to me how surprised they are that I haven't yet written a column about my now two-week-old daughter. I assure them that it's certainly not because her birth, which I was extremely involved with, wasn't utterly miraculous. Nor is it that her presence, which I marvel at for hours on end, isn't absolutely awe-inspiring. Neither is it that the reality of this new being, this marvel of creation, hasn't significantly increased the joy and wonder of life and love for both me and my lady. It's just that it's all been so intensely private and personal, and I have wanted to keep it so. It's something I haven't *wanted* to put into words. Mostly, because I haven't wanted to sound like a blithering, blathering, babbling, baby authority, and another annoying new parent. So I have held off ... until now.

And what, you may wonder, is the insight that has made such an impression on me, the emotion that has moved me so deeply for me to now feel like I have something worthwhile to offer? It is this – that *babies are like golf.*

The thought occurred to me today when my lady, the mother of this wonderful child, remarked, "It's amazing how one little smile can make all the rest disappear. All the discomfort and difficulty of getting the nursing thing together, all the three a.m. feedings, all the dirty diapers, the re-working of our schedules all becomes, not only totally worth it, but forgotten each time you see that little face light up."

That's when I heard myself say, "It's just like golf," and what I meant by that is that all it takes is one good shot to keep you coming back. You can hack around all over the course, but if you hit just one really good shot, it looks and feels so good it makes you think that next time maybe you can hit *two* good shots.

And if you believe that, then you also believe that, with enough practice, you can hit 'em all good.

Of course, experience and observation suggest otherwise, for even the best players among us still flub shots, and still make mistakes in judgment and execution, and they still have poor rounds and bad days (as do babies). And even though they (the golfers, and parents for that matter) have plenty of knowledge that is supposed to help keep them from making mistakes, nevertheless, mistakes still continue to happen.

That's the frustrating thing about golf – just when you think you've got your game pretty much under control, suddenly it's out of control.

Which is another way that babies are like golf, for just when you think you've got a particular "skill" mastered and a particular "problem" handled, and that you're past that, sure enough it pops up again and keeps you up most of the night. Or keeps you from arriving at your appointment on time, Or from planning things out in advance. The point is, even the most mellow, well-behaved babies are still going to have their moments when they blow up.

The challenge in golf as with babies is how do you respond once the disturbance occurs? Do you keep your composure or do you fall apart?

Which leads to yet another way that babies can be compared to golf. Players who are passionate and philosophical about the game of golf contend that there is probably no greater teaching device on earth as far as revealing aspects of themselves. I have only been a parent for a couple weeks and I am already aware of how great a teacher my daughter is and will be for me. I am convinced that she is here to teach me as much, if not more, as I am to teach her.

Another, though completely mundane, similarity that can be drawn between babies and golf is that they are both expensive. Yet, in both instances, if it is something you love then you never even think twice about spending the money because the joy you derive from it is so worth the cost.

I'm sure that if I took a little more time I could continue to draw all sorts of parallels between babies and golf, but as I sit here and watch Tiger Woods hold on to win the final PGA Championship of the 20th Century, I am satisfied that my little glib comment does, indeed, have some degree of truth to it, and so I shall enter it into the Book of Theorems, Maxims and Postulates that I have compiled along the way, along with such veracious observations as: *"Untuned cars are erotic aids,"* and *"If you want to get something done, turn off the TV."*

August 17, 1999

Why shouldn't I feel good ...it's still early

I was out of my gourd with glee this morning. For one thing, my wrecked ankles felt a whole lot better than they did yesterday. Don't know why they felt so bad yesterday, or why they felt so much better today. But they did, and that feeling of wellness had me springing and bouncing into my day.

It was gray and misty as I set out from my home, and I savored the feeling of the fog as I climbed into, and minutes later, out of my truck. Through layers of new day.

And I banded together with a hundred other boys and men whose hearts were ignited, whose eyes were sparkling and whose muscles stretched and fired in the dampness.

And, thankfully, I was outside watching it all when the sun broke through, and the clouds dissipated, and brightness and blueness then took over the sky.

Yes, and then, with still half the morning left, I found myself doing something I hadn't done in years. I climbed a tree. Now I don't mean I just pulled myself up on to an easily reached branch and hung there for a minute, I mean I jumped, clutched, pulled, hung, swung and *climbed* up a good distance into a tree. Don't know what compelled me to do so, but there I was, disregarding the ants, sitting patiently on a branch, waiting to startle the passers-by whom I knew would soon be arriving, for they were my reason for being there.

And when I came down, though I haven't fully come down from it yet, I walked among the nature 'til I reached my truck, and then headed off into the workaday world, armed with the things-to-do list I prepared last night before bed.

And bang, ... one two three, and eventually, seven eight nine, I checked off each of the things on the list.

And when I strolled into the office, my liveliness and merriment could not be contained, and one of my co-workers asked and wondered, "What happened to make you so happy?"

And as he turned to answer his ringing telephone, I paused, and regarded my gladness ...

... I walked her out to the parking structure, mostly just to be polite. We hugged, for I'm a hugger. The hug turned into a kiss. The kiss turned into a passionate, poetic moment. The moment endured.

I visited, and never left.
I traveled, and saw it all.
Met every kind of person in every kind of place.
Got filled with a sense of purpose. And a sense of wonder.
Saw myself and my aspects re-emerge
Found a new home, a new beauty, and a new way of looking at it.
Made some new friends, and mostly kept the old.
Beheld many a miracle.
Wrote it down and had it read.
And received.
Had a child.
Counted my blessings.
Found love ...

... And as he hung up the phone, I answered, "Nothing in particular," for the way I saw it, it wasn't that something specific had happened to make me feel happy today, although climbing that tree worked wonders, it was more a matter that nothing had *yet* happened today to *keep* me from feeling my happiness.

"The world gets better every day – then worse again in the evening."

> - Frank McKinney Hubbard

Aug. 25, 1999

He weren't no saint,
but he's one of mine

Even though no one ever officially canonized her, to me, my grandmother was a saint if ever there was one. Which reminds m e ...

...When I was a kid, we used to have a St. Christopher medal clipped on to the visor in our car. It was a protective measure. St. Christopher was the patron saint of travelers, and the patron saint of travelers is supposed to take care of people on the road.

I say St. Christopher *was* the patron saint because in 1969, he got stripped of his sainthood. The Catholic Church took a long look at all the saints on its calendar to see if there was historical evidence that the saint actually existed and lived a life of holiness.

In doing so, they determined that much of the information, and a lot of the stories, about many of their "saints," including Christopher, were based on legend.

In the case of "the martyr formerly known as St. Christopher," the legend goes something like this: He was born somewhere around the 3rd Century with the given name of Offerus.

After growing to extraordinary size and strength, Offerus resolved to serve only the strongest and bravest.

He pledged his allegiance first to a king, but when he found out that the king was afraid of the devil, he switched his allegiance to Satan. Until he found out that the sight of the cross frightened Satan.

Finally, a hermit convinced him to offer his allegiance to Christ. The hermit baptized Offerus "Christopher," which means *Christ-bearer*, and gave him the task of carrying people across a raging stream.

One day, he was carrying a child who grew heavier and heavier. Alas, the child got so heavy that it seemed to Christopher like he was holding the weight of the whole world on his shoulders. The child made himself known as the Creator and the Redeemer of the World, and to prove his statement, he ordered Christopher to plant his staff into the ground. The next morning, it had grown into a palm tree. The miracle converted many non-believers, which enraged the ruler of the region. Christopher was thrown in jail, and after much torture, was beheaded.

Well, all this happened, if it happened at all, a long time ago. The Church couldn't prove any of it, even though there is plenty of evidence that the guy named Offerus/Christopher did actually exist. So without proper proof, they decided to un-canonize him, leaving Raphael the Archangel, Nicholas of Myra, Anthony of Padua and Joseph as the remaining patron saints of travelers.

But I've got my own patron saint of travel. It occurred to me, last week at 3 a.m., as I was driving to the airport to go catch a plane to hook up with some of my cronies in the old stomping grounds. The thoughts, the words, and especially the feelings were already starting to flow, as I began fumbling around in the dark, searching for a pen and some paper and the switch to turn on the overhead light. When I found each, I wrote:

My patron saint of travel is Jack Kerouac

What I meant by that is that every time I break away from the day-to-day routine and get out, especially out of town, and let clocks and schedules fade away and people and places come alive and matter more, I feel *guided* by the *spirit* or the *feeling* I get from Kerouac's stream of consciousness writings.

And I pray that I may fully experience the experience; that it might touch – really touch - my awareness; make me come alive, and more alive; that it etches itself into my memory, and that it goes into and comes out in my writing.

It's realizing, like Elvis Costello sang, that "Everyday I write the book." And that the book is the story of my life, and that *that* is certainly not already all said and done, unless I stop living and loving and striving to express *IT*.

A patron saint can be thought of as a "guardian" of a place or an activity. For me, when that place is "on the road," and when the activity is "traveling around, experiencing *IT* and expressing *IT*," one of my chief guardians is Kerouac. And while he was certainly no saint, he was, most definitely, an angel. A desolation angel.

September 1, 1999

Making a molehill out of a mountain

There's this bit you see in a lot of TV shows, for those who watch a lot of TV shows, where someone who's having to deal with some kind of dilemma or situation says: "I saw a similar thing in a movie one time, and what they did is ...," and then they tell, or show, what the person or persons in the movie did, and that becomes the basis for the solution to their situation. The suggestion is that by knowing and remembering how some-one else dealt with something can sometimes be helpful as far as how you choose to deal with the same or a similar thing. And so, it is because of that suggestion that I'm going ahead and sharing what I re-learned today for what must've been the umpteenth time.

First off, let me begin by saying that the past week was prob-ably the busiest one I've had, or will have, the entire year. There's no need to go into the details of why I was so busy, but suffice it to say that the past, the present, the future, personal and profes-sional, work and play, art, sport, family, friends and finance seemed to all converge within a few day period, and the one thing that there was just way too little of, was sleep. And I started stressing over all that needed to get done.

What I noticed, was that the more I worried about what had to get done, the less I actually did. It was like I was getting in my own way, and tripping over myself.

And I knew that what had happened was that I had allowed the task at hand to become too enormous. It's like the way that some people conceive of the great work of changing the world. That is, by changing every thing and every person, rather than one thing and one person, namely themselves, at a time. One step at a time, one day at a time, which, as the bumper stickers say, is the way that people who are working to overcome their addictions systematically reclaim the responsibility for their lives.

The thing to keep in mind is that it takes energy to do anything at all. In physics, we speak of potential energy and kinetic energy. In the sphere of human performance and achievement, I offer up the concept of *assisting* energy and *resisting* energy. Through the use of mind and will and outlook you can use your energy to assist in the performance and execution of the task, or to resist and oppose it from getting it done. In other words, you can be part of the problem or part of the solution.

One way to go about doing this is to take a difficult or even seemingly impossible task, and reduce it down to a series of much easier and definitely possible tasks. We often hear of someone making a mountain out of a molehill. Well, this technique involves **making a molehill out of a mountain.** By doing so, that which is impossible becomes less and less so, while the realm of possibility grows ever greater.

I dwell in Possibility
A fairer House than Prose –
More numerous of Windows
Superior – for Doors
        - Emily Dickinson

So, next time you feel yourself feeling overwhelmed by the task or tasks at hand, may you recall the technique of "whittling it down," that you may deal with it more effectively and with less anxiety.

Oh, and one other thing to keep in mind when you feel anxiety building, don't forget to breathe, for breathing circulates a fresh flow of energy. Conversely, interrupting your breathing cuts off the flow of energy, and as I said before, energy is needed to do anything and everything.

Clearly, there is nothing I've said here that is new or original. I offer it, primarily, as valuable reminder to myself. But, if the earlier suggestion – the one that says knowing how someone else dealt with something can be helpful when it comes time for you to choose how you're going to deal with the same or a similar thing – proves true, then perhaps you may remember and find this helpful.

"Take it easy,
Take it easy,
Don't let the sound of your own
wheels make you crazy."
- Frey/Browne/Souther

Sept. 7, 1999

Take two Bob Marleys and call me in the morning

Upon waking, I could already tell something was going on. I had a heavy head and a sour stomach, and I could feel the fever coming on, but there was no time for any of that, for we had to get going.

The feeling of physical funkiness continued to build and spread as we wound our way over the hilly highway. I was breathing deeply and deliberately, trying to draw in some kind of restorative force. Then, I flicked on the radio. It was the Sunday morning "Breakfast with Bob" show, which is a one-hour program featuring the music of Bob Marley and the Wailers, and after just one verse of the first song, which happened to be "Roots Rock Reggae," I could already feel a slight change taking place. The pressure in my head was beginning to ease up just a bit, and I felt fresh air, or fresh something, coming in from somewhere. At the same time, the sun began to break through the morning clouds of fog. By the chorus, I was singing along in full voice, and clearly feeling a bit better.

The next song, which I also sang along with, was "No More Trouble," and with that one, the sourness of stomach began to mellow.

By the third song, "Kaya," I was amazed at how much better I was feeling, and I recalled the line, "Music hath charms ..."

I was particularly blown away by the speed with which the music was working. I mean, if you take a pill for your head or stomach ache, you likely have to wait 15, 20 minutes or so before the thing kicks in. The music was helping me immediately.

Now, it's no mystery that music has healing power, which is

why classes in music therapy are now offered at colleges, universities and medical schools across the country, and around the world. Most of the time, they focus on emotional and mental healing, and since our physical health is tied to our emotional and mental well-being, the music therapy ends up spilling over into a form of physical healing.

I've brought up the subject plenty of times in interviews with musicians, and they, too, for the most part dwell primarily on the emotional and mental aspects of a song, and what it can do to your mood. They point out how different songs and different sounds affect different people differently. But what they are describing is the subjective power of music, and not some sort of objective force. Not that I think it invalidates the power of music to talk about subjective effects, it's just that I suspect that there is an objective power to music as well.

For instance, if you talk about penicillin, you can say that it destroys bacterial infection. Or take, say, ibuprofen. It's widely referred to as "an anti-inflammatory."

In the case of music, my suspicion is that the objective power has to do with the vibration.

By vibration, I don't mean just the physical vibration associated with blown air, a plucked or bowed string, or the reverberation of a surface such as a drum skin or a piano string that has been hit. Nor am I referring only to which key the music is played in, though these things, indeed, have a bearing on the vibration. By vibration I mean the energy of consciousness and the effect of divine activity. Vital to the vibration of the music is the *intent* of the composer and performer, as well as their talent and awareness.

Which made me wonder whether it was the power of music, or whether it was the power of Bob Marley music, in particular, that had me feeling like I was healing. To test it out, I changed the song by changing the station, and I can say that, for me, the other music wasn't having nearly the same affect.

I say "for me," so does that, imply, subjectivism? Maybe, and maybe not. For instance, it is popular these days to speak of "the Mozart Effect," which suggests that listening to the music of Wolfgang Amadeus Mozart stimulates higher brain function. This is especially true, say the researchers, for infants and young children. Other music, including other great classical music was tested, but there was something special about Mozart's music. Perhaps it was his inherent understanding of the objective power of music.

When we more fully understand this power then we can truly begin a new age of healing through the use of music.

I can imagine it now – hearing our doctors and healers say things like: "Get some rest, drink plenty of fluids, and listen to Van Morrison;" or "Try two Bob Marley CDs and call me in the morning."

September 15, 1999

Moving beyond this or that to this and that

Two elderly men approached the booth, and looked at what I was selling. One of them picked up the book, flipped it open to the index, and started skimming through the titles. Noticing the second one on the list, he asked, "Why do you say that 'Skepticism never gets us any further than we already are'?"

I didn't remember, offhand, the specific details of the essay, but I was pretty sure that the point I was trying to make, and I told the man this, was that the thing that often keeps us from realizing and experiencing new possibilities is our own sort of arrogant insistence that we already know full well what is and what is not possible.

He asked me to give him my definition of a skeptic. I didn't attempt to offer some concise dictionary definition, nor was I about to try and encapsulate what I think the adherents of the philosophical school of *skepticism* believe in, but I did mention something about "doubting things," and "playing the devil's advocate."

"Isn't that a good thing," he asked. "Wouldn't the opposite be blind faith?"

Sensing where he was going, I said, "Just because I happen to note that clinging to our established beliefs keeps us from gaining new insights and understanding, doesn't mean I'm saying that we shouldn't question things."

And then he said that the difference between scientists and artists is that scientists are skeptical, while artists operate on faith.

I thought, not only is that an inaccurate characterization, but it would suggest that we have to be one or the other, and the same way all the time. As if we're not allowed to be skeptical in some situations and at other times operate on faith. I rejected the suggestion that one must be "either this or that."

Later, another man came up, thumbed through a few pages, and then asked me what I call myself. I thought - I must've looked, to him and to others, like a dog reacting to a high-pitched noise - you know, tilting my head one way and then the other, trying to understand what I'd just heard. Until he indicated that he was referring to *liberal* versus *conservative*, and he was wondering which one was I.

If you look up *conservative* in the dictionary, or at least in my dictionary, the first thing it says is "one who opposes change." But Life is constantly changing, so if we were to adhere to the dictionary definition then it would seem to suggest one who opposes Life. And I would hope that's not me, therefore, I would never use that word to describe myself.

Looking up liberal in that same dictionary, I find that it says "progressive, broad-minded, tolerant, generous." I certainly aspire towards each and all of those qualities, but still, I wouldn't use that word to describe myself. Not only because it doesn't apply in each and every situation, but because I reject labels in general. They are simply too limiting.

(A thought occurs to me here - wouldn't someone who is both liberal and conservative be even broader-minded than someone who is just liberal?)

And it didn't stop there ... for soon I was facing a man who asked if I am, and if I call myself, a Christian. For me to say so would almost be like identifying myself as "an eater of green leafy vegetables." Sure, it's true, they make up a major part of my diet, but that's not *all* I eat. I explained that I get my food and understanding from various sources, and that I try and integrate the various teachings and the various examples of love and compassion.

Another man, who was standing off to the side, stepped in and said, "I've been standing here listening to what you were saying, and I liked and agreed with everything you said up until that last part."

"Which was what," I asked.

And he remarked, "There's only one God."

"I agree," said I.

And he went on to talk about a triune deity, which I also agreed with.

And then, it was he who looked like the confused dog, as he wondered aloud, why then I wouldn't call myself a Christian.

And the first guy asked, "So then are you new age?"

As if those were the only options ...

To me, a *new age* implies a new way of communicating, a new way of getting along with each other, a new way of accessing our power, and it isn't mutually exclusive of belief in God, or Christ, or Allah, or Buddha, or the sun, moon and stars.

I found it surprising that that many people would have such a need to label things. As far as I can tell, saying what something is, calling it something, rarely gives an understanding of what and how the thing really is.

Take water, for instance. We can say that it is a liquid. Yet under certain conditions it is a solid, and in still other situations it is a gas. It's the same with people. We're not just this or that, and always the same.

If we are to arrive at a greater understanding of truth, then, perhaps, we need to bring ourselves beyond labels, and beyond the notion of this *or* that, to a concept of this and that, which is bigger *and* more inclusive.

September 20, 1999

Take it where you find it; songs as a source of information

"Thanks for the information."
— Van Morrison

Every once in a while, you learn something that's really useful. Like a couple weeks ago, when my sister-in-law was over making dinner. After peeling off enough leaves of lettuce for our dinner salad, she put the rest of it back in the refrigerator in a plastic bag along with a paper towel to absorb the moisture, which is the great wilter of lettuce. And it's amazing how well it worked.

I tell you this because for the past few years, one of my pet peeves has been how I've not been able to keep red leaf lettuce in the refrigerator for even a few days without it turning brown. Now, just by sticking a paper towel in the bag, I'm able to keep lettuce for a week-and-a-half if I want.

I wonder why this paper-towel technique is not more widely known. It seems like somewhere along the line it's something I should have learned or been taught. Was there no teacher of mine that knew this ... and why doesn't the supermarket have a little sign over the lettuce display letting us know it?

Which brings up the question of *where* and *how* we get our information.

First off, we get it from those in our environment; from our parents and family, our friends and our neighbors. We get it from school; from our teachers and our fellow pupils. We get it from what we read, watch and listen to. From who we run into along the way. We get it from dreams, from inexplicable impressions, from unmistakable signs.

Many of us in the rock and roll era have acquired a great deal of information through the songs.

I think of the factual, historical-type of things I've picked up. Like – when was the Battle of New Orleans fought? I know, because Johnny Horton sang: *"In 1814, I took a little trip, Along with Colonel Jackson down the mighty Mississip."* I know, thanks to Gordon Lightfoot, the name of the giant iron ore freighter that sank in the Great Lakes, which lake it sank in, and what the Chippewa Indians call that big lake. And I know, from Dylan, who killed Hattie Carroll, and once found guilty of the murder, how long of a jail sentence he got.

But historical tidbits are just a small part of the valuable information I've received through songs.

Some people scoff at the idea of learning anything of real value from a pop song, and that to rely on singers and songwriters for such information results in a warped sense of reality. But as Van Morrison sang, on his "Wavelengths" album: *"You take it where you find it."*

For instance, I might have turned to Thomas Carlyle to read, *"Blessed is the man that has found his work,"* or I could have studied the words of FDR, to hear that: *"Happiness lies in the joy of achievement, in the thrill of creative effort,"* but instead, I got the same message from Van Morrison, who sang: *"If you live the life you love, You get the blessing from above,"* and in my opinion, Van's phrasing of it is much more powerful. Or, I might have learned a lesson from Oliver Wendell Holmes, who wrote: *"To keep your secret is wisdom; but to expect others to keep it is folly,"* but I learned the same lesson instead, from Bob Marley, who sang: *"Only your friend knows your secret, so only he could reveal it."*

Had I read more of the philosophical works of Cicero, I

may have formed the opinion that *"Avarice, in old age, is foolish; for what can be more absurd than to increase our provisions for the road the nearer we approach to our journey's end?"* but I came to that conclusion anyway, helped in no small part by John Lennon, who sang, *"Last night, the wife said, Oh boy, when you're dead, You can't take nothing with you but your soul."*

"You can't always get what you want, But if you try sometimes, You'll find you get what you need;" *"Only love can conquer hate;"* and *"You don't need a weatherman to know which way the wind blows;"* None of these are less powerful testaments of truth than, say, *"What goes up must come down,"* *"A penny saved is a penny earned,"* or *"There's nothing to fear except fear itself."*

... Or, for that matter, that putting a paper towel in a bag full of lettuce will help keep it from wilting.

September 22, 1999

Sticks and stones and old crane bones

I read this article today in one of the scientific journals about what they called the "oldest musical instruments in the world," which were found not too long ago at an excavation site in China. The instruments, made out of crane bones, are these 9,000-year-old flutes. As I am naturally interested in the origin of things, and the first this and the oldest that, I was drawn to the story.

The flutes, which have five, six, seven or eight holes, are based on a seven-note scale. Our standard Western diatonic scale is an eight-note scale. The scale describes a relationship of energies or sounds. Different scales describe different relationships, as well as different sounds, which is why, for instance, that it is difficult for a lot of "Westerners" to listen to "Eastern or Middle Eastern music." It's because the relationships and the intervals of the sounds are just a bit too awkward for their conditioned minds.

We know the world sounds different today than it did before, just by virtue, if nothing else, of all the motors and electric lines. But it's not just the sound of the machine that is different. I had a guy urge me, one time, to check out the voice and the manner of speaking of the actor Edward G. Robinson. Many of us are familiar, as his is a popularly-imitated voice, with how sharply he spoke and how biting his tones were. But, as the guy who urged me to check it out pointed out, that's actually how people sounded in the 1930s, when Edward G. was making movies. That was 70 years ago (as I write this.) Imagine how they sounded 9,000 years ago. Very different, I'm sure.

As I was reading the article, I found myself feeling somewhat surprised that the oldest instrument would be a flute, until it said "the oldest multi-note musical instrument." The reason I was surprised has to do with the techniques we have for making musical sounds. In general, we beat, we blow, and we pluck or strum in order to create musical sounds. It would seem to me that the most primal of these sound-creating techniques is *beating*. Thus, I would think that the oldest musical instrument would be a drum of some sort. And that's when it hit me. And that's when I thought, in particular, about Roberto.

He's a musician in the true sense of the word. He exists to make music, and everything he sees becomes an instrument of his expression. On his recordings, as well as in live performance, he uses everything from fruit to combs to condoms to make music, as well as more traditional and more respected instruments.

The Greek conductor Dimitri Mitropolous, who worked mostly with a *12-tone scale*, said, *"I live with music like a monk who prays every moment."*

It describes what I mean about Roberto, and the other great musicians I have had the honor and pleasure of hearing, knowing and traveling with. Music is in their soul, and they play it as necessarily as do they breathe. Which, I realized, is why it's futile to try and identify, and also ridiculous to go ahead and designate, something as "the world's oldest instrument," unless you're willing to include sticks and stones.

And then there's the matter of deciding *what is* and *what is not* music. I think here about the people who, in commenting upon whichever current style of music bugs them, say, *"You call that music?"*

And while it might be neat to know what was the first music, who were the first musicians and what it was they played, I'm much more interested in feeling music, and understanding the role music plays and has played in the evolution of humanity and the unfoldment of consciousness on this planet.

"Music is the universal language of mankind."

- Longfellow

"There is music even in the beauty, and the silent note which Cupid strikes, far sweeter than the sound of an instrument. For there is music wherever there is harmony, order, proportion; and thus far we may maintain the music of the spheres."

- Thomas Browne

October 7, 1999

Slavery, prostitution and seduction

On the long drive back home I was listening to the radio in my truck and my attention was struck by two commercials, which came on one right after the other. The first one had a guy who's supposed to be a "success expert," and he was hawking a tape called "Selling Yourself in the New Millennium." As for the second one, I didn't even catch what it was supposed to be selling, but, in its inane way, it drew upon the story of the Sirens, those sea nymphs whose hypnotic music lured sailors to their death.

While the first commercial was still playing I thought, *didn't it used to be that the noble and respectable thing was to not sell yourself,* as in to not sell out, to not sell your body or your affections, or to not sell yourself short. I reminded myself that the only people who *are sold* are slaves, and those *who sell themselves* are prostitutes. And though I know it was talking about the nuts and bolts of making a positive impression upon someone so that they will give you something you want, such as a job or money, I also saw that as long as it is framed within the context of someone being bought and sold that it is, wittingly or not, promoting slavery and prostitution.

As they were announcing the address and phone number for how and where to order the tape, I started singing the verse from Dylan's "Idiot Wind" that goes:

"You close your eyes, and part your lips,
And slip your fingers from your glove,
You can have the best there is,
But it's gonna cost you all your love,
You won't get it with money."

The second commercial then came on, and when they brought up the story of the sirens I started thinking about the seduction of the sailors, and how they were drawn in until they crashed into the rocks.

The rocks, it seems to me, were but a metaphor for *materiality*; that is, that which you can see and touch and adequately describe. But if material-mindedness is the surface upon which we crash, and get disrupted in our journey, then what, I wondered, could we look at as being the siren's song that lures us in?

My first thought was that the sirens are our strong desire for security. We think, I think, that financial soundness brings greater certainty into our lives, as if it can alleviate a person's fear of the unknown. We think that material security can deliver us from pain. And while it is true that there are certain basic hardships which are almost certainly averted when one has a roof over one's head and food in one's belly, still, one has to learn to deal with heartache and suffering and pain of another sort.

And it was there, as I was refuting whatever power security might have in assuaging our fears, that I realized there is a yet deeper impulse pulling us into the treacherous rocks of material-mindedness. It is the belief in the separate self.

When we conceive of ourselves as existing separately from all the rest, it is then that we set about looking out for number one rather than looking out for each other. It is then, also, that we become more concerned with staying out of harm's way than we do with spreading harmlessness. There's plenty to worry about when you start to worry about me me me. You worry about not getting what you want, or about losing what you already have. The sense of the separate self is the breeding ground for our fears.

If, on the other hand, we could keep in mind that "I am He, as You are He, as You are Me, as We are All Together," then we could alleviate not only the fears of pain and the unknown, but others too, such as fear of failure and even fear of death.

He or she who lives free of fear is slave to no one. And he or she is no one's prostitute.

So when you start to hear the voice of the separated self singing songs of isolation, turn your ear, instead, to the rumble of the waves, to the whistle of the wind, to the heartbeat of the world and to the cries of your brothers and sisters, all of which keep you far enough out in the cosmic sea so as to avoid the disruption and the destruction.

November 21, 1999

On how we learn and the value of memory

When I'm working on the computer and there's something I don't know how to do, which is often, I ask someone who does know, or who I think might know. Luckily, and thankfully, I am surrounded by people who know more than I do and who are willing to share their time and knowledge with me. Occasionally, though, someone will hand me an instruction manual, and invite me to wade through the pages upon pages and find the answer for myself. In such instances, I usually give it a shot, do exactly what it says to do, or so it seems to me, and after getting nowhere except to the point of frustration I abandon the idea and go an entirely different route.

It's not that I can't learn things through books. I've learned plenty in that way. Enough to get college degrees in physics and psychology, and plenty other things of value and importance to me. But there's something about the instruction manuals that just doesn't click.

According to a research scientist at the University of Wisconsin, who apparently is causing somewhat of a stir among researchers in his field, it's not my fault.

"Those instructions run counter to how your memory works," says psychologist Arthur Glenburg.

When I read that, it reminded me of a Michael on Fire lyric that goes:

"You're not crazy,
And you're not lazy,
And you're not weak, you're strong.
Everything you do is right,

It's just the world that's all wrong."

Glenburg argues that psychologists should drop the current widely accepted view that human memory works like a computer. He claims that memory is the direct result of action, of how the body moves and responds to its environment, and he claims that action-oriented learning can improve the teaching of technical information. By "action-oriented learning" he means information that is somehow connected to an experience or a memory.

In my case, for instance, I definitely learned how stupid it is to be a midnight nuisance when that guy got in his car and chased me and my friends, some of whom *were* being midnight nuisances, and he pulled out a gun and threatened to kill us. And I learned how important it is to switch over from "DC" to "AC" when you pull a Leisure Van into a campground and plug it into the power outlet, especially if you're going to grab hold of the medal ladder that's attached to the back door of the van. And it took some time but I even learned not to leave my feet and go for my friend Tom's head and ball fakes if he's inside of 18-feet and hasn't used his dribble yet.

But I don't see what's so radical about that. Teachers and coaches have always known that you can't just tell your pupil something, or even have them read it, and then expect that they know it. You have to tell them, show them and then have them do it in order for them to learn how to do it.

"In the case of following instructions," says Glenburg, "the trouble stems from trying to draw on memories we don't have yet."

Now, that sounded a little more radical.

Glenburg calls his theory "the embodiment theory." His contention is that for knowledge to be useful it must be "embodied" within a memory.

There are others who feel that "embodiment" is probably the greatest barrier to knowledge. Such people maintain that in our original unembodied state, that is, before we are born, we are pure consciousness, and that in that state, we know and understand all there is to know. The task once we descend into these physical forms is to remember what we already know, including our own true nature.

December 7, 1999

New Year's and 'now' are filled with hope

"... It was the triumph of hope over experience."

- Samuel Johnson

Despite Bono's contention that "nothing changes on New Year's Day," I'm inclined to think that maybe something does change, even if it's something you can't see, touch or pay the rent with, and even if it only changes a little bit.

I call it hope, but I'm not talking about optimism here. Nor is it so much about positive thinking.

It's more like a kind of confidence. Like the kind of poise you might have if you were on your way to get a second root canal. Sure, there might be some trepidation about having to go through oral surgery, but having been through it once before you know you can deal with it. *You can do it*, in other words.

Or in another sense, like the kind of confidence you might have while driving over a twisting turning mountain road after you've done it several times before. After you've gotten to know the turns and the switchbacks, and after you've learned when you can speed up and when you should slow down, and when you have to stay tight and when you can take it a little bit looser.

Similarly, when another year rolls in like a wave coming off the sea of uncertainty, you can stand firm knowing that it's not going to topple you over and carry you out to sea. On the contrary, you might even be able to catch a few good ones breaking, and ride 'em on in to the firmness of the shore and the promise of a waking dream.

It's an interesting hope, for though it is of the *mind*, it works hand in *hand* with certain qualities of the *heart* to produce wishes, create trust and maintain belief. Wishes that hold the prospect of fulfillment. Trust that the laws of physics and of cause and effect are not going to just all of a sudden go crazy on you. Belief in your potential and in the potential of others.

As far as why it happens at New Year's, I think it's just because it's such a convenient marking point. It has more to do with the *measurement* of time than the *movement* of time; movement in time. For instance, most of us are able to say where we were and what we were basically doing last New Year's Eve. It's not so easy with dates like April 21, June 7 or August 12, which may hold special significance for some people but for the most part are not particularly noteworthy. Jan. 1, though, is such a clear line of demarcation. The place at which next year and last year converge and in which this year emerges is the boundary that marks the end of the old and the beginning of the new.

If we call "the old," instead "the past," and rather than "the new" we say "the future," then it is easy to see how New Year's is a celebration of "now."

"*Life is real,*" wrote Gurdjieff, "*only when I am.*"

Not when *I was*, not when *I will be*, but when *I am*, which is always *now*.

Now is the only time we can do anything. We can not do something in the past and we can not do something in the future. And even though in the future we might be able to do something, maybe even something we did in the past, when we do it, it will be now.

Which is another reason why I say hope rises at New Year's, for "now" is filled with hope. Alive with potency and possibility. Free from the shackles of yesterday's shortcomings. Unencumbered by tomorrow's expectations.

So, as I sit here and begin to clear away the holiday cards

that bear "best wishes" from our friends, and hopes for a joy-ous New Year, I will, instead, send out hopes for the now and all its freedom, along with a wish that you may have the confidence of a second root canal (without having to go through it), and the ease that comes with knowing the road.

December 29, 1999

Ask not what a politician can do

Hadn't been up for too long this morning when I flicked on the tube. I tuned in just as the news anchor-person was report-ing that the formidable former (and maybe future) candidate, the wife of an even more formidable former candidate, has pledged her support to the current candidate in the future elec-tion. In citing her reason for coming out on his behalf, she men-tioned, among other more substantial things, that "he can re-store pride to the people of this nation."

Now, maybe it's a streak of cynicism setting in here, but my first reaction was, "What are you talking about? What the heck could any politician do to make me feel proud?"

I mean, yeah sure, in an abstract sense, there are definitely some benevolent human-rights kind of things ... Or, I don't know, maybe give the Indians back their land, or subsidize the artists, or put food coloring into the jet fuel so that amazing streams of color will trail in the wake of our high flying machines, but I don't really see any of that happening.

I guess it's just because I get moved more by things that occur on a smaller, closer level between people. Like community, for instance. People cooperating with each other not because it's been legislated, or mandated or regulated in any way, shape or form, other than within the private chambers of one's own conscience.

It's a funny thing, pride. It's like fire, you know; one thing if you've got cold soup and green wood on hand but something entirely different if there's dry, brittle wood.

We try and instill it into our youth. I know, as a coach, I try to get the players to take pride in the effort they put forth in all areas all the time, even when there's no one watching.

We give awards for pride.

We stress civic pride, and school pride, and national pride...

And yet, we are told that pride is first among the vices. That pride comes before a downfall. CS Lewis called pride, "the complete anti-God state of mind."

And that's why it's tricky.

Not too long after this morning's newscast, I got to reading this book I've been visiting for a few minutes a day, lately. I was reading about the great 20th Century lyricist, Yip Harburg, who wrote the words to such classics as "Brother, Can You Spare A Dime?" "Paper Moon," "April in Paris," "Lydia, the Tattooed Lady" and "Somewhere Over the Rainbow."

Harburg said he wrote "Rainbow," and all the other songs in the "Wizard of Oz," as a metaphor for the Franklin Delano Roosevelt era. He made reference to FDR's "Four Freedoms" speech, pointing out that the President's plea to have "freedom from want," and "time for learning and for arts" became the

Scarecrow's: "My head I'd be scratchin,' While my thoughts were busy hatchin,' If I only had a brain."

Roosevelt's call for a Good Neighbor Policy became the Tin Man's, "If I only had a heart." And the line about, "The only thing we have to fear is fear itself" became the Cowardly Lion's: "And I could show my prowess, Be a lion not a mou-ess, If I only had the nerve."

Harburg was noted (in the Brahms and Sherrin book "Song By Song") as saying: "In spite of the Depression [FDR] gave us inspiration – new light that gave the people social security, old age pensions, unemployment insurance, and that sweet new feeling of togetherness."

Certainly, not everyone was or is so approving of FDR, but what was quite clear to me was that within Harburg's remarks lies the answer to my earlier question ... that the way a politician can make us feel proud, is by giving us a feeling of togetherness. And if a politician, any politician, can do that then more power to him or her. But I don't need the President to do that for me, I need only to walk around town, and meet with my neighbors, and speak with my compadres, wherever they may be.

In that famous "Four Freedoms" speech, Roosevelt called for "freedom of speech," "freedom to worship" in whatever way one might choose, "freedom from want" and "freedom from fear."

Roosevelt said, "It is not a vision of a distant millennium. It is a definite basis for a kind of world attainable in our own time and generation."

Well here we are, maybe not in some distant millennium, but at least in the next millennium, even if we're talking about another year away, and we still have people who can't or don't express themselves for fear of being persecuted on a lot of different levels. We still have people who can't or don't openly worship in the way that they choose for fear of being hounded and threatened. We have a ton of people who are slave to their economic situations, and who, regardless of whether their country is at war or not, never know a day of peace. And, yes, there is still plenty of violence and aggression, but it's getting better and we're going in the right direction, towards freedom.

With a new year starting and everyone making resolutions, perhaps freedom is one we can all resolve to pursue more vigorously. And I don't mean just some vague notion of freedom at large that depends on government and military, but a freedom that each individual takes responsibility for having a stake in.

As FDR said at the close of that speech, "Our strength is in our unity of purpose."

January 5, 2000

They belong with us, and with us may they stay

Mention the name Pittsburgh, as in, say, "Pittsburgh Steelers fan," and it connotes an image that is "blue collar, hard-working, and as American as apple pie."

Not surprising, then, that the man whom many consider to be "the great American songwriter" was born in Pittsburgh, though at the time it was called Lawrenceville.

I'm talking about Stephen Foster, who was born on the Fourth of July (1826), unlike another self-proclaimed Yankee Doodle Dandy, George M. Cohan, who *liked to say* he was born on the fourth, but was actually, if my memory serves me well, born on the third. Another difference between the two is that Cohan, as we know him through his work, was red, white and blue all the way. His songs were overtly patriotic and nationalistic whereas Foster's were and are universal; great songs that just happen to sound, feel and be uniquely American.

Songs like "Old Folks at Home," or as it's also called, "Way Down Upon de Swannee Ribber." Others include "Oh! Susana," "Camptown Races," "Beautiful Dreamer," "Jeannie With the Light Brown Hair," "In the Merry Merry Month of May" and "My Old Kentucky Home."

I've been noticing myself singing a lot of these songs and melodies lately. I might not know all the words, though I know some of the words to each one of them, but I can hum them, for many were taught to us in school. As for the others, which I somehow know though they were never taught to me, they just seem to blow through the breezes and flow in the streams. And when I do look to find the words to his songs, which is easily done, so significant to our make-up are they, I am left even more in awe.

For instance:

"I sigh for Jeannie, but her light form strayed,
Far from the fond hearts round her native glade;
Her smiles have vanished and her sweet songs flown,
Flitting like the dreams that have cheered us on and gone,
Now the nodding wild flowers may wither on the shore,
While her gentle fingers will cull them no more:
Oh! I sigh for Jeannie with the light brown hair,
Floating like a vapor, on the soft summer air."

Nothing overtly American about those words, and yet put them together with their well-known melody and it's hard to imagine them being written or sung anywhere else but on a porch or a parlor somewhere in America.

Or how about:
"Way down upon de Swanee ribber,
Far, far away,
Dere's wha my heart is turning ebber,
Dere's where de old folks stay.
All up and down de whole creation,
Sadly I roam,
Still longing for de old plantation,
And for de old folks at home."

According to the American Music Center, "Old Folks at Home" is sung in almost every language known to man. But again, this song about the return of the prodigal son is quintessentially American.

"Swanee River" is the official state song of Florida. Foster also wrote the one Kentucky chose as their state song ("My Old Kentucky Home.")

Though he left us with so many national treasures, Foster died broke and penniless at the infamous Bellevue Hospital in New York. While staying at some rundown dive hotel, he became feverish and ill. After days of lying alone in bed, he apparently went to go clean up at the wash basin in his room when he got light-headed and fell, bashing and cutting his head on the sink. He lay there and nearly bled to death, until the maid found him the next day. An ambulance came and took him to Bellevue, but he was too weak from the fever, and he had lost too much blood. He never recovered, and on Jan. 13 he died at the age of 33.

But his songs remain. Here we are, 150 years later, still singing them. Some people deride these songs for being too simple, but to me, the genius of them exists in the simplicity. It's like they were floating around in heaven, and Foster brought them down to us on earth. They represent the perfect marriage of words and music. It is a mystical union that joins thoughts and feelings, the material and the spiritual, the temporal and eternal.

Foster's songs are part of our psyche. They belong with us, and with us may they ever stay.

"Sooner or later that which is now life shall be poetry, and every fair and manly trait shall add a richer strain to the song."
- Ralph Waldo Emerson

"Now, good Cesario, but that piece of song,

That old and antique song we heard last night;
Methought it did relieve my passion much,
More than light airs and recollected terms,
Of these most brisk and giddy-paced times:
Come; but one verse."

(Shakespeare in Twelfth Night, Act II. Sc. 4)

January 12, 2000

Peace in our time,
how about peace in our lives

"We realize that the peace we enjoy is the absence of war rather than the
presence of confidence, understanding and generous conduct."

– Raymond Gram Swing

Too often, when we think of peace it is in relation to war, which suggests grand-scale conflict between nations or races or other large groups of people. The thing with grand scale, though, is that it implies "big" and "far away." But what about the small and up close kind of conflicts? Small, maybe, in the grand scale of things, but not to us as we're going through them.

Do we think along the lines of peace when it comes to the confrontations that pop up in our personal and professional lives? Is that grand and noble theme with us or is it more a practical case of holding our tongues so as to not upset the apple cart? Or denying our hearts so as not to ignite a spark that might set off a powder keg? Or disregarding what we think, or even what we know? Even if we don't know *how* we know it.

Or, on the contrary, do we spit on our hands and dig our heels into the ground and raise our voices and puff our chests out to repress any perceived opposition or unpleasantness?

Do we try and invoke pity?

If we approach peace using the old dominance-and-submission stratagem then it is a shaky peace at best. An unstable and deceptive peace. And though it may appear to secure calm within the palace there is discord within the walls.

The case of the self-divided. Like when the heart says one thing and the mind says another. Or when circumstances indicate one reality but the soul yearns for another.

Something here

We hear of the peace process, and of envoys who negotiate peace. We, too, within the context of our personal lives, are often impelled to negotiate peace. The value of negotiation is not necessarily that it teaches us to give up or give away something we want, or even *some things* we want so that we can get *other things* we want. Rather, that through it we learn to recognize and let go of that which we don't really need.

We, meaning you and I, are unable to go make peace with a country or with "a people," but we can make peace with our neighbor, and be at peace with ourselves. And that is the challenge of being a peace-maker.

Some of the greatest peace-makers the world has ever known have given us a "technique" for making peace. It is the philosophy of non-violence.

Another word for non-violence is harmlessness, which I like because it carries the connotation not only of harm in the physical sense, but includes also the notion of harmful thoughts and words.

Some have referred to the non-violent approach as a form of civil disobedience. Others have called it passive resistance. Gandhi, who was one of its great proponents, rejected both phrases because, in his view, there is nothing passive about creating peace, nor did he consider peace-making being disobedient. He searched for another word, but he couldn't find a positive, active English word to describe the philosophy. So instead, he chose the Sanskrit word "Satyagraha," which means "the pursuit of truth."

"The way of peace is the way of truth," he wrote. *"Truthfulness is even more important than peacefulness."*

Truthfulness begins with looking in the mirror, and noting our positive and negative qualities. Looking is a first step, seeing is a next. Accepting is yet a further step and appreciation another still.

"Peace cannot be kept by force. It can only be achieved by understanding."
> – Albert Einstein

"Nothing can bring you peace but yourself; nothing can bring you peace but the triumph of principles."
> – Ralph Waldo Emerson

January 18, 2000

Questions regarding the conversion of energy

$E = mc^2$ sure has been on my mind a lot lately. In this eloquently stated relationship it is revealed that energy is neither created nor destroyed, only changed from one form into another. It seems to me that if you give any serious thought to what that means then it's inevitably going to force you to ponder our origin, our nature and our destiny, as I did on my walk the other day.

But before I got to all that, I started thinking about energy here and now and in our everyday lives. According to the equation, we can't "create energy." Yet, I've definitely experienced having been "pumped up" and "energized" by someone, and also having "pumped up" and "energized" others, haven't you? The conservation theory explains that that *energy*, that *feeling, wasn't* created. Something else, some words or perhaps a thought or feeling, was *converted* into that energy.

For me, it brings to mind a saying that hangs from many a-locker room wall, the one that goes: "Enthusiasm creates momentum." It becomes enthusiasm *is converted into* momentum. Enthusiasm, a mental state, is converted into momentum, a form of energy. I've observed it in action, and if it's true then it affirms that thought and energy are interchangeable, as are mass and energy.

We can ask ourselves, does this mean that thought can be converted into mass? Must we now recite another equation that deals with the relationship of thought and energy, perhaps an E = tc2, or can we just expand the concept of interchangeability?

Next, I considered what happens in the realm of artistic creation. It becomes artistic *conversion*, suggesting that, in truth, we don't *create* works of art, rather we transform something else into art. I once described it as "metabolizing experience."

All of that fit, well enough for me, into $E = mc^2$, so I continued on, along the sidewalk to my further ruminations.

It occurred to me that, I think, most of us think we can go back to the beginning. But according to this very basic law of physics, this so-called universal law, there was no beginning. Energy is and always has been. So what does that do to science's most popular and accepted explanation for how the universe began, namely the Big Bang theory? It says, guess what guys, there was energy even before there was a big bang, so the big bang wasn't the beginning.

The other question is what does it do to our concept of God? A first look suggests that if $E = mc^2$ holds, then God couldn't have created the energy because energy cannot be created. Upon further inspection, though, we find that energy, while infinite in terms of time and duration, is finite in other ways. The fact that it is conserved, and that it cannot be created or destroyed, means that there is a definite amount of it. Also, consider this. The universe is the domain of all that is. Beyond the universe there exists nothing, not even energy. But still, the universe, though constantly changing, has dimension. It is bounded, and thus finite. God, on the other hand, by almost any definition you care to look at, is infinite.

So while our science may not be able to prove an omniscient, omnipresent and omnipotent God, neither does it refute One.

Having looked back, I then looked forward to consider the question of what happens when you die. Answer: *You don't die.* $E = mc^2$ says you are *converted* from one form into another. Mystics consider whether or not we can maintain continuity of consciousness through the conversion process. Some say it is a matter of keeping our memories intact. Others say the answer is in a new equation that relates consciousness and energy.

January 25, 2000

Singing a song about the blues

I was thinking earlier today about possessions, and how they can clutter up a house or a life. It occurred to me that our most prized possessions are the ones we'll never have to worry about fitting into a drawer or a closet or a storage bin, and what I was thinking about when I was saying that to myself was the "stories" that we carry around with us. The memories.

My treasure chest is filled with tales from the road. Filed by the names of the towns, each with it's own cast of characters. Names like Huntsville, Grand Junction, Dubuque and Kalamazoo. Similar, in a way, to such notorious names as Lexington and Concord, Saratoga or Bunker Hill, for they were the battle sites in my own private war for independence.

Like all soldiers in all wars we claim freedom as our reason for fighting, but judging by the body's bondage it must be a freedom of spirit and expression that we restlessly pursue.

The badges earned in these skirmishes cannot be worn upon the lapel, and yet they are just as evident. Let's see, this one here is for all the missed birthdays and weddings and funerals. All the places you woulda been if you coulda been, if you only coulda got there. This one's for all the times you sucked it up and poured it out in a near-empty barroom, and this other one over here is for all the lesser rooms you filled up in the middle of the week in the middle of nowhere. And then there's one for all the broken-down vehicles, and the broken-down equipment, and this tattered one over here is for being broke period; for coming home with pockets that are just as empty as when they left.

Throughout this century, American troubadours have left home and taken to the road like soldiers going off to war. Men and women who have paid a heavy price for authenticity, and who have sacrificed themselves, their comfort and their security, so as to inject something into a song that you just can't get any other way.

In the eyes of some they are but loafers who have shirked responsibility and who lead, or have led, lives that leave a lot to be desired. Some do, and some have. And yet, without the ones who have roamed and rambled and put themselves out on the front lines, vast regions of our own territories would remain unrevealed to us.

The record of their trials and travails are splattered across the roads and through the alleyways. The true triumph is that they can somehow set our hearts on fire and uplift our spirits.

The great gift of "the blues" is that it gives us a way of getting inside and beyond our sorrows and our heartaches.

The story of the blues is our story, indeed. Let us honor those who have told it truthfully.

"We all know that our bluesmakers of all folks cannot possibly be ranked like football teams or mutual funds. I think, in fact, that we'll never know who the truest bluesmakers were or where they came from. Consider the West African griots or that itinerant bluesman that W.C. Handy found and lost at the Tutwiler train depot in 1903. Consider all the Henry Sloans we've never heard and the mothers of those we have. And consider the folks whose paths never crossed those of the white historians or those who sang only to themselves and their God."

- Curtis Hewston

January 26, 2000

I repeat, consistency has its place

I was talking the other day with the father of one of the brightest stars around on the high school sports scene, and he was explaining his continuing involvement in his kid's athletic development. He said, "By this point, I've taught him pretty much everything I know, and that I used to do, and now it's just a matter of continually feeding him balls. Repetition, that's the most important thing."

Whether it's shooting free throws, putting golf balls, or playing scales on a musical instrument, the key to mastering complex motor performance skills is repetition. Doing the thing over and over again until it becomes natural, and can be done without even thinking about it. It's a process of removing our own mental and psychic obstructions.

"It is not, 'I am doing this,' but rather, an inner realization that 'this is happening through me,' or 'it is doing this for me.' The consciousness of self is the greatest hindrance to the proper execution of all physical action."

- Bruce Lee

Another value of doing something over and over is that it helps you develop a motion, a stroke, that is the same all the time, so as to minimize variance and inconsistency. The idea is that repetition leads to consistency, and consistency translates into competence, reliability and proficiency.

The idea of consistency — I was thinking about it earlier in the week during one of my workouts. I was remembering back when I used to work in the health club, and there was this guy with these incredible abs who used to spend almost all day every day lounging around the pool. He hardly ever even stepped foot into the gym, and yet he had totally cut ripples. I asked him what he did to have such a well-defined stomach, and he said, "I do 75 sit-ups every morning."

"That's it?" I asked, incredulously.

"That's it," he said, "but the key is consistency. A lot of people get all hyped up and go gung-ho for awhile, and then they stop doing it, and then they start up again when they feel like it. You never get anywhere that way. I only do 75 sit-ups, but I do them each and every day, no matter what."

I reminded myself that these same principles hold true not only in regards to physical tasks but also when it comes to the development of mental and psychic faculties as well. I was thinking about prayer and meditation, and while I believe in spontaneity and the power of the Spirit to bring about any kind of result at any given moment, it is, I thought, rare that a person develops a keen sense of intuition, or a conscious realization, or is able to transcend the limitations of time and space, such as the reports of those Tibetan yogis seen flying over the monastery walls, without working at it diligently over time.

I decided to look in the large, popular book of quotations to find an inspirational excerpt on *repetition* or *consistency* that might help spur me on in my daily practice. Surprisingly, almost every single thought and saying gathered there, put forth by people who obviously took the time to ruminate and comment upon these topics, spoke about repetition and consistency in negative terms. They mostly had to do with how repetition serves to turn us into robots, and how even the mere attempt to do and treat things the same way from day to day locks us into set, all-too-familiar forms and patterns that tend to rob life of it's freshness and aliveness.

One need only consider the examples of some of the great technicians in their fields, such as the Larry Birds, the Ben Crenshaws, the Arthur Rubinsteins, to see and realize that there is obviously great value in applying repetition to your training, and striving to attain a high degree of consistency. At the same time, I am reminded of all the graduates from the most venerated music schools and institutes I've known who have become adept at technique yet have been unable to express themselves. Then again, I've known others who've gone through and come out of such programs who are masters of expression.

It's a fine line, or as some say, a razor's edge. Freedom of expression, in the arts or in sports, requires the development of skills and "licks" so that you have the ability to actually pull it out and pull it off when the moment arises. At the same time, there needs to be an abandonment of style and training so that you are not limited by what you've learned, so that you don't just keep automatically reverting to the same chops over and over again.

Again, I turn to Bruce Lee, who, in commenting on "the formless form" remarked: "Expression is not developed through the practice of form, yet form is a *part* of expression. The greater (expression) is not found in the lesser (expression) but the lesser is found in the greater. Having 'no form,' then, does not mean having no 'form.' Having 'no form' evolves from having form. 'No form' is the higher, individual expression."

February 8, 2000

Dreams, dreaming, dreamtime and aspiration

So as to spur us on to attempt, and maybe achieve, something great, we are often encouraged to keep our dreams alive, or, said another way, to hold on to our dreams. This suggests that dreams can endure over time. Interestingly, though, the longest dream ever recorded lasted but two minutes and 23 seconds. That was in 1967 in a laboratory in Chicago.

Now, obviously, there's a question of semantics going on here. In the first case, the word *dream* refers to a *hope* or a *goal* while the latter usage pertains to a cycle of sleep, the so-called REM or rapid eye movement cycle. When we speak of dreams in this context, we are referring to the stories or the sequences of events that unfold during this stage of sleep.

Researchers have observed that the rapid eye movements, the active brain waves and the increased breathing that correspond to our dream state occur, in infants, during 50 percent of the sleep period. They've found that, in general, the amount of time spent in dreams decreases steadily until the age of 10 or so, and then remains pretty much constant at around 25 percent from that point on.

If that's true, and if, say, seven hours of sleep is about average, then that means that an hour and 45 minutes each night is spent dreaming. If the longest one is 2:23, then that means we're having at least 50 dreams a night. Most people are doing good to remember even one or two of them.

"Dreams," sings David Gates, in one of the huge hits by his group Bread, *"are for those who sleep.*

And, *"Life,"* he points out, *" is for us to keep."*

Dylan says pretty much the same thing on his "Slow Train Coming" album, when he sings, *"You got some big dreams, baby, but in order to dream you gotta still be asleep."* And then he goes on to ask, *"When you gonna wake up?"*

The insinuation in each of these two cases is that to call something a dream is to suggest that it is but a wish or a flight of fancy not made real by one's actions and decisions.

Which is why when we were out there day after day, week after week, year after year, traveling around, and someone would say, "You're so lucky to get to live your dream," we would, some of us, reply, "This isn't a dream. This is my reality. This is what I do."

Lately, it sure seems like I've had a lot of people talking to me about the *significance* of dreams. In an interview I conducted recently, a doctor/healer brought up the idea of receiving information from what people into Jungian psychology might call "the collective unconscious," or what many indigenous tribes might call our "ancestors," but what he called "the field." He compared it to the aboriginal concept of "dreamtime."

The Aborigines of Australia call it "Tukurpa," pronounced *jook-oor-pah.*

Dreamtime refers to *the time before time,* or *the time of the Creation,* and *dreaming* means simultaneous existence in the past, present and future.

In Castaneda we're told that, *"Dreaming has actually nothing to do with dreams. Its ulterior purpose lies in shifting and moving the assemblage-point and by so doing the Dreamer awakens the Double and is able to perceive facets of reality that lie beyond reason's ability to comprehend.* **Dreaming is the vehicle that carries the Dreamer into the unknown** *and that which is witnessed there can only be experienced, not talked about in other ways than telling Tales of Power."*

In other words, the power we derive from dreaming comes not from analyzing our dreams but from accepting them without accepting them and disregarding them without disregarding them. Which, I think, is why I always appreciated Dylan's lines from "Gates of Eden," where he sings:

"At dawn, my lover comes to me
And tells me of her dreams,
With no attempts to shovel a glimpse
Into the ditch of what each one means."

Because the Unknown is huge and wondrous and magical, whereas the analytical manner of talking about it, about dreams, seems always to reduce them to intellectual blah-blah.

As for the matter of keeping our dreams alive, would that we could say the right thing at the right time so as to keep each other empowered. In order, though, to avoid the non-affirming connotation of dreams as mere airy wishes I like to use, instead of the word *dream*, the word *aspiration*. So, while we use *dreaming* as a vehicle into the unknown, let us aspire to the pursuit and realization of noble ideals and the steady expansion of consciousness.

February 15, 2000

Treating ourselves
as good as we do our things

I bought this great new laptop computer. What makes it great is that it allows me to be mobile and still get the work done.

It can run on battery power for a couple hours, but after that I have to plug it into a wall socket to charge it up again. I let it run all the way down one time when I first got it because the instruction booklet that comes with it says to do that. Since then, though, I've been very careful about not letting it run too far down because I rely on it, because what I do with it is important to me, and because I wouldn't want it to not be there when I need it.

So after using it to write for a couple hours during our drive up north the other day, and plugging it in as soon as we arrived, I caught myself snickering and asking myself if I care more about the computer, and if I respect *it* more than I do my own body, mind and spirit. What I meant is that *I would never even think of* letting the battery on the computer wear out, and yet I regularly let my own battery run down by going way too long without sleep, by working (indoors and sitting down) for long stretches, day in and day out, without "plugging in" and charging back up.

It's ludicrous to think that I might treat my computer better than I treat myself, but I figure that I can always somehow handle it, for, unlike the computer, I have the capacity of being able to breathe deep and draw in the cosmic substance that renews and restores me. That alone keeps me from running down more than I do. Still, there is no excuse for any of us to think, say or act like we don't have the time to do whatever it is that we like to do to fortify and rejuvenate ourselves, when in reality, if we took the time to do it, it would make everything else better.

The act of "plugging in" to the boundless source of energy, the universal force, the stuff that is in all stuff, is probably about the best thing you can do for your health and well-being, your wisdom and understanding, your relationships, your expression, your path and your power. So how can there not be enough time for that which is "probably about the best thing you can do?"

And the thing is, it doesn't take *much* time. It's not like you need to get out of town or take a vacation or spend a lot of money to recharge your battery. You just need to let things go for a minute, and allow yourself to experience some of today, this day, and be alive without getting overwhelmed by all your perceived responsibilities.

Oh, the times I've arrived at this same place and this same realization before. When I do, I usually go for weeks and months keeping it a priority. Keeping the realization that taking the time to plug in makes me so much better. I'm there now, and I pray I can maintain the energy and awareness, and the sense of humor too, to make it last.

March 15, 2000

Spring and Aries and the Journey to the East

Glancing up at the calendar that hangs on the wall behind this computer, and noticing that today's date is clearly marked with the words "Full Moon" and "Vernal Equinox," I am reminded that it is now officially springtime. Not that I needed some piece of paper to clue me in to the fact that the weather's changing and the world around me is waking up. There's plenty enough evidence to indicate that. Like, for instance, the hillsides covered with the bright hues of wildflowers, the morning chatter of the birds, or the heightened restlessness I see in the teenagers hanging out around town. For me, though, the most clear pronouncement of it occurred a couple nights ago when I was standing out on the train platform and I felt thrilled and soothed at the same time by the warm wind kissing my face.

As it is these days, the first day of spring happens on the last day of Pisces. It wasn't always that way, though. It used to be contained in the time period corresponding to Aries, but because of the phenomenon known as precession, that is, the slow change of direction of the Earth's axis with respect to the stars, the vernal equinox gradually moved into Pisces. If we manage to survive and hang around long enough, it will eventually move into Aquarius, which is the sign that comes before Pisces.

Pisces is considered the last sign of the Zodiac, and Aries is the first, so in that regard it can be described as the end of one cycle and the beginning of another. Many of us who like to think that a brighter day and a higher consciousness awaits us tend to want to say that kind of thing all the time – that it is the end of the old and the beginning of the new - but here's one place, one time, one of many, that is, in which it is convenient to proclaim it. Perhaps, then, it is worthwhile to give some consideration to Aries.

Aries is represented by the ram. In Greek mythology, it relates to the story of the golden fleece.

According to the story, Mercury, the messenger, gave a magic flying ram to this woman Nephele when her husband took a new wife, Ino, who persecuted Nephele's children, Phrixus, the boy, and Helle, the girl. To keep them safe, Nephele sent Phrixus and Helle away on the back of the magical ram, who flew off to "the East." Helle fell into the Hellespont, now the Dardanelles, which is that ribbon of water separating the European continent from the northwest portion of Turkey. Phrixus made it safely all the way to Colchis on the eastern shore of the Black Sea.

On arriving at Colchis, Phrixus was welcomed by the King, whose name was Aeetes. As an offering to the king, the ram was sacrificed, and its golden fleece hung in the sacred grove of the war god, Aries, where it was guarded by a huge dragon.

Later on, Jason and his Argonauts embarked on the great Odyssey, or journey, to find and get the golden fleece. And therein, I believe, lies the significance of this time period.

Though it would be foolish and way beyond the scope of my understanding to even attempt to put forth information that sounds like a "reading" or a commentary that applies to large groups of people the world over, I do think that there is a timely pertinence in speaking, symbolically of course, about making the "journey to the East" to get "the gold."

I've always understood "the East" to mean "where we go to get wisdom." Thus, to speak of a "journey" to the East is to describe a conscious and purposeful pursuit of wisdom and greater understanding. And "gold" ... well, gold is what you finally find there in the East. It is the great reward for untiring effort and unselfish service. Some call it virtue, some freedom, some describe it as an awareness, while still others give it the name — wisdom.

As for where we may find it, I recall the words of William Blake who, in "The Price of Experience," wrote: "*Wisdom is sold in the desolate market where none come to buy,*" which brings to mind the Dylan lyric from "Idiot Wind" that goes: "*You can have the best there is but it's going to cost you all your love, you won't get it with money.*"

Thus, it comes down, once again, to an admonishment "to love." It is the wise thing to do, and it will yield the greatest reward.

March 19, 2000

On the value of mnemonic devices

Had somebody ask me how many days there are in the month, so I proceeded to fold my fingers into a fist with my knuckles pointed skyward and, with the index finger on my other hand, I started counting. The person looked at me, and asked what I was doing.

"I'm counting the months," I explained. "The months that fall on a knuckle have 31 days, and the ones that are in the valleys have 30 days, or in the case of February, 28 or 29 days."

My friend had no idea what I was talking about. He had never come across, what for me is, the surest and quickest method of knowing how many days there are in the various months. What I do, is start at the knuckle on the baby-finger, and call that January, and then I start making my way towards the index finger. February is in the first valley, the ring-finger knuckle is March, and since it's on top of the knuckle that means it's got 31 days, the valley between the ring and middle fingers is April, indicating 30 days in that month, and so on and so forth. That means the knuckle at the index finger is July, and since it's on top of the knuckle that means 31 days. From there, you can either cross over to the other hand or start over again from the beginning, either way it's the same.

That's how I was taught to remember how many days the months have, and since it's totally reliable, I don't bother to remember it otherwise.

Counting your knuckles is an example of a mnemonic device, that is, a trick or a system that helps you remember something. Like "Every Good Boy Does Fine" helps us remember the notes corresponding to the lines on the treble clef, or like "ROYGBIV" helps us remember the sequence of the colors of the visible spectrum.

Considering how effective mnemonic devices are in helping us remember and retrieve various odds-and-ends type information, it would seem mighty worthwhile for us, similarly, to develop little aids or systems to help us remember really important things.

I know one guy who keeps an old shoe in his office as a reminder to himself that he should always try and see things from "the other person's" perspective. Or, said another way, it's a reminder for him to always try and walk a mile in the other guy's shoes. I know another guy who has a tattoo of his mother on his arm that serves as a continual reminder of how much she had wanted him to get a college degree.

Sometimes, a simple mantra, like, for instance, Paul Atreides' "Fear is the mindkiller," or Bobby McFerrin's "Don't Worry, Be Happy," can serve as an effective mnemonic device. Some people *wear* things, like a chain or a medal, or a crystal or a badge or a button, while still others perform some gesture or gesticulation, such as the sign of the cross.

Just as there are different "themes" for different months, that help us remember to, say, eat healthy or get our blood pressure checked or read to our children, likewise, I'm always coming up with different themes for mnemonic devices to help me keep my awareness focussed.

I've used words like "SPEAK," which was a self-admonishment to Spread Power Energy Awareness and Kindness, I've had "HAY WAY AWAY GO" taped on to my dashboard, which reminded me to ask myself "How are you? Where are you? And what are you giving off?" and I've used "TIT FOR TAT," which simply pointed out that "There is a force of redemption that's always there," and that kinda helped keep me from getting overwhelmed by things that would pop up during the course of the day.

In addition to words and phrases, I've also resorted, from time to time, to doing little things with my fingers that no one else could see, but which held meaning for me, and I've used a visual image, such as the sight of the mountain looking out from my driveway, to remind me that "there is always something higher."

These three techniques – using words, pictures and kinesthetic sense – make use of the three main learning and memory styles.

I highly recommend mnemonics as an aid in "remembering." Of course, it is up to each individual to decide for themselves what is important to remember. Once that's done, you can either make use of other people's existing tricks, or make up some of your own. Just make sure it's something that has meaning for you, and that you're comfortable with. Don't worry about it sounding too weird, chances are, the more peculiar the device the more powerful an aid it will be.

March 22, 2000

Worry belies belief in God and science

Sometimes, a little knowledge can be a dangerous thing. For instance, knowing how much you have to do, and how much time you have to do it in. Especially if it seems like there's much to be done and not much time to do it in.

What often happens to me, and what I see happening with others, is that I, and we, tend to get ahead of ourselves. That is, we focus on the whole big thing rather than just plodding ahead with one little bit at a time. And the trouble with that is that the whole big thing can tend to be overwhelming.

Allowing our minds to drift ahead to all that has yet to be done and all that needs to be done takes away from the time that could be spent doing it.

Thankfully, I've come to recognize this. Not that I don't still succumb to this habit of getting ahead of myself, it's just that when it does happen, I usually can notice it happening, and just by virtue of noticing it I'm able to pull myself back so that it doesn't wind up being too debilitating.

Lately, when I notice it, I've been using two simple reminders to help me flush away my worry, and get me back in a more relaxed frame of mind, to the task at hand. The first reminder is that the journey of a thousand miles begins with a single step. The other is a lyric from a Peter Tosh song that goes: *"Now that you find yourself with your back up against the wall, One step towards progress and I know Jah will help you all."*

These two statements tie together nicely because not only do they point out the obvious – that in order to finish first you have to get started, but they go on to say that once you do get started, somehow the task will get a little easier.

Tosh's explanation for why it gets a little easier is that God helps those who help themselves. This calls on us to have some faith. Or, perhaps, by buying into it we build faith.

It occurs to me, though, that there is a physical explanation that further supports these statements. The explanation I'm talking about is Newton's First Law of Motion, which says that a body at rest shall remain at rest, or if it is in motion then it shall continue to move at the same speed and in the same direction unless acted upon by some force. The force, in this case, is the force of our own mind. If we can overcome our own anxiety about doing something, and actually get the ball rolling, then the motion should continue to proceed relatively smoothly provided we can keep our minds from stopping the motion.

I bring this up only to point out that stressing out over the load is not only an act of self-sabotage that significantly decreases our productivity, but it is also a faithless act that belies the belief in divine assistance and in the laws of physics.

When it's put that way, I feel kinda foolish about getting bogged down as often as I do.

"Anxiety is a word of unbelief or unreasoning dread. We have no right to allow it. Full faith in God puts it to rest."

– Horace Bushnell

"There is noting that wastes the body like worry, and one who has any faith in God should be ashamed to worry about anything whatsoever. It is a difficult rule no doubt for the simple reason that faith in God with the majority of mankind is either an intellectual belief or a blind belief, a kind of superstitious fear of something indefinable. But to insure absolute freedom from worry requires a living utter faith which is a plant of slow, almost unperceived growth and requires to be constantly watered by tears that accompany genuine prayer."

– Mohandas Gandhi

Some people claim that what you don't know can't hurt you. While I would not wish to espouse the virtues of ignorance, yesterday I observed how *not* knowing kept me from getting overwhelmed.

We were in a town we'd never been to before, staying in a hotel, without a car, and our daughter came down with "a condition" that required a curative, and, because of why we were there I only had an hour in which to get it. The concierge gave me directions to the closest place he thought might have what I needed. Having just watched a movie about the late great Steve Prefontaine, I took off running, in search of the apothecary. Along the way the directions got jumbled and jarbled and I never did find the names of the streets he told me to look for. So I just kept going.

Had I known, in advance, how many miles I eventually wound up going, I wouldn't even have attempted it. I would've called a taxi. But as it was I pulled it off and never once worked against myself.

I did it by just putting one foot in front of the other, and by just continuing on until I got to where I needed to be. No worries, No fears. And that's the attitude I shall strive to maintain as I continue along the path of my personal unfoldment.

March 28, 2000

Holding out hopes
of finding a gem among the junk

It wasn't a big city or a small city, more like a big town, and as we drove through and around it, we noticed yard sales and garage sales at what seemed like every third or fourth house, every block of the way.

Who, I kept asking myself, are they selling to? The answer was obviously themselves, for there weren't any tourists hanging around. And whatever outsiders were there on business weren't,

I'm quite sure, gonna be stopping on those raggedy streets and avenues when there were plenty of nicer and safer places to be.

There were several times, while stopped at a stop sign, that I took good long looks to see what kind of things were selling. I recall spotting some old scraped and dented pots and pans, some well-worn auto tires and wheel rims, some old clothes hanging on wobbly racks.

All they're doing, I remarked, is exchanging each other's junk. And as it all finds correlation in a song, I soon started singing:

"Motor Cars,
Handle Bars,
Bicycles for two,
Broken-hearted jubilee
Parachutes,
Army Boots,
Sleeping bags for two,
Sentimental Jamboree.
Buy, buy, says the sign in the shop window,
Why, why, says the junk in the yard."

- Paul McCartney
"Junk"

There was so much junk.

I truly couldn't believe the number of rummage sales I saw everywhere. My initial tendency was to shake my head in disgust, but even as my head was shaking, I realized what do I care what others are doing and why should I feel a need to think or say that there's something wrong with it. I suppose it's just because I feel much too much clutter in my own space.

Nevertheless, I tried figuring out what could compel all these people to spend their day there hoping for passersbys to stop. The thing that came to mind was my own recycling routine. I know recycling is ecologically a good thing to do, and that's all the reason I need for doing it, but still, I take my trash over to the recycling center in the next town rather than the one in this town because I get a few bucks for it there.

And then I recalled that great bowling shirt I wore through the 1980s. I bought it at a yard sale, because it had my name embroidered on the front pocket. But that's not all. It had this big brightly-colored, intricate picture stitched on the back of the shirt. At the top of the scene were the words "Rice Paddy Daddies," which, apparently, was the name of a bowling team out of one of the U.S. military bases in Southeast Asia. I thought it looked pretty cool, and it fit great, so it became and remained a popular part of my wardrobe for a number of years. Eventually, it fell out of my starting lineup, and when I no longer wore it much at all, I was getting ready to give it to the needy, when I fell in love, and instead gave it to my gal because it had my name on it. It was like giving her my class ring or my "letter sweater," which, for those who are too young to remember, is something that sweethearts did back in the middle of the 20th Century. She kept it around for a while, and then eventually we packed it up in the bag of clothes we gave to the Salvation Army. I've often wondered if someone's out there walking around with that shirt on, and even how I might react if I saw it.

And I thought, too, of the old book on alchemy, purchased also at a yard sale for a mere dime. As one of the most treasured ones in my collection, it's there always at my bedside in the pile of my dozen or so most special ones.

And suddenly, I was on the other side of the fence, figuratively speaking, appreciating what people might get from these sidewalk sales.

I used to know this old guy who would walk down the street

and intentionally drop coins along the way. Then, he'd wait in hiding to see people find the money and take it. In his mind, he was giving more than the amount indicated on the coin, he was spreading around hopes and dreams of something more and something better.

Maybe all the yard sales I saw is an indication that a lot more people these days are out there trying to simplify their lives. Maybe it's some kind of an ecological anti-corporate revolution. Or maybe it's just an indication, and I take great heart in this, that there are still plenty of people holding out hope of finding a gem out there among all the junk.

April, 2000

In the Land of the Jazz and the Home of the Blues

... "As American as apple pie."

How about "As American as jazz and blues." For, while people all over the world appreciate, and also create, jazz and blues music, nevertheless, jazz and blues are distinctly American art forms.

And since we seem to have managed to create all kinds of holidays to celebrate any and everything under the sun, and since

April 4 happens to be the birth anniversary of both Duke Ellington and Muddy Waters, each of whom are most definitely among the greatest of the greats in the realm of jazz and blues respectively, I've decided to proclaim and celebrate today as National Jazz and Blues Day.

Now I am certainly no expert on either of these guys, and neither do I claim to be some kind of musical scholar who can tell you what it is and what it all means. I have, however, had my emotional and intellectual horizons broadened by the both of them, and that alone is worth paying homage.

When I was growing up, big band music, which is primarily the format that The Duke played in, wasn't really something that young people listened to. I listened to rock and roll and folk music, and the jazz I did get into was generally the avant-garde sort played by smaller combos.

In 1976, Stevie Wonder, who is someone I was majorly inspired by at the time, wrote and sang: *"Music knows it is and always will be one of the things that life just won't quit, But here are some of music's pioneers that time will not allow us to forget, There's Basie, Miller, Sachimo, and the king of all Sir Duke."*

Stevie said it, and I didn't doubt it, but still, I didn't go out and start listening to Ellington's music.

Then, last year, I had the good fortune and great opportunity of interviewing Ray Charles, himself a member of the Rhythm and Blues and the Jazz Hall of Fame, as well as the Rock and Roll Hall of Fame, and a performer often referred to, simply, as "The Genius." I asked Ray who he thinks are the true geniuses and whose music he thinks will stand the test of time. Without a moment's hesitation, Ray answered, "Duke Ellington," whom he considers the greatest of them all.

Then, a couple months ago, I read a self - interview Duke

Ellington did with himself, and it was the best interview I think I've ever read. It totally turned me on. Every statement was as profound as Lao Tzu, or someone like that. So I started listening, and – wow!

In the case of Muddy Waters, born McKinley Morganfield, again, it was other artists who I love and listen to that instilled a reverence of him. Especially The Rolling Stones, who even took their band name from one of his songs.

But it's not because I think that these guys are great that I think we should have a Jazz and Blues holiday. It's because I sincerely believe our music has contributed as much to the freedom and spirit of this country as any political movement or military force or religious group or business organization.

I was even thinking that, just as it's mandatory for kids to learn about George Washington and Abe Lincoln, Alexander Graham Bell and Thomas Edison, Harriet Tubman and Martin Luther King, Jr., or any of the other significant figures in American history, so too should they learn about cats like Duke Ellington and Muddy Waters. Some people might think that's totally ludicrous statement, but I dare say that the music sung out in the fields on the plantations freed more slaves than Abe Lincoln or any legislative act ever did, or could. And that our music has done more to promote international relations than Ben Franklin and Henry Kissinger combined.

The reason we don't, learn about Duke Ellington and Muddy Waters in school is that, unlike apple pie, which is considered wholesome and promoting of family-values, jazz and blues music is kind of dangerous and non-conforming. But, you know what, so is freedom and so is bravery.

Jazz music is the epitome of the First Amendment of our Constitution, for at its very essence is the freedom of expression. And Blues, well, to me, that's a whole way of dealing with the hand life has dealt you. It's a way of getting past your problems and facing your worries and your fears. And isn't that what bravery is all about?

Which is why I proclaim today National Jazz and Blues Day.

I think I'll celebrate it by listening to the music of Duke Ellington and Muddy Waters.

April 4, 2000

The ABCs of practical math

Here's one for you – a practical example of how the transitive property can be used in our everyday lives. For those who don't remember from math class, the transitive property says: if $a = b$, and $b = c$, then $a = c$.

Now here's what got me thinking along these lines today. I happened to come across this quote of Confucius that said: "There are three marks of a superior man: being virtuous, he is free from anxiety; being wise, he is free from perplexity; being brave, he is free from fear."

Being familiar with the language of Confucius, as it has been translated into English, I am aware that when he speaks of superiority, as in "the superior man," it is not in relation to the realm of outward or worldly affairs. It's a way of talking about our higher and better selves.

And so, it struck me that here were instructions, broken down into three specific exercises or techniques, for anyone wishing to realize his or her higher and better selves.

In all three exercises, the "a" in the equation is "the superior man," which, of course, also is "the superior woman." In the first exercise, "b," according to Confucius, is "virtuous." Leaving us with the equation "the superior man" = "virtuous."

Well, if we leave it at that, it's kinda like Nancy Reagan's "Just Say No" slogan. It doesn't really help. Just as saying to someone, "If you want to realize your higher self then just be virtuous" doesn't really help. Which is why we introduce a third value — "c."

In this case, "c" is "free from anxiety," and that seems a little more tangible, something we can check ourselves on.

If we can bring ourselves to the point of conceiving how the transitive property could possibly hold true in the realm of human consciousness and behavior, then we see that "keeping ourselves free from anxiety is one way of realizing our higher self."

I say one way because Confucius then goes on to give us two other ways.

But let's stick with the one way for a moment. If we choose to do this exercise in earnest and really put forth an effort into seeing what kind of results it yields, we will inevitably be thrust into a serious study of, in this case, anxiety. We will consider what happens to our body, and how, for instance, it signals us, when anxiety starts a-creepin' on in. We will ask ourselves what is it that we are anxious about, and how does our behavior towards other people, especially our loved ones, change when we *are* anxious.

We might, for example, notice that we hold our shoulders

up, or that we suspend our breathing when anxiety starts to set in. We might realize that we get impatient with people when it starts to build up. Or that we get defensive.

And so we start paying attention to those things, and as our understanding of our anxiety grows, so too does our proficiency at keeping ourselves free from anxiety. The more "free from anxiety" we find ourselves, the less impatient shall we be, since that is one of the outcomes of our anxiety. It follows that the less impatient we are then the more patient we become, and, as we all know, patience is a virtue, which is the "b" in the equation ... and that's how this whole thing works. By focusing on "c" you become "b," and by becoming "b" you attain "a."

Considering, now, the other two techniques given to us by Confucius in this specific statement, the "c" in the second one, namely *perplexity*, isn't a particularly helpful value to me. Which reminds me to point out that the transitive property can be extended out how ever far you need to take it in order to create a meaningful relationship for you personally. For instance, we can introduce a "d," say simplicity, and by focusing on that value, we connect ourselves through the successive stages and successive values right on up to "the superior man."

The crux of it, of course, depends on whether the statements hold true, that "a" actually does equal "b," and that "b" really does equal "c." I know, who's to say what's true and what's not? But the point is, just because you say $3 = 4$ doesn't make it so. Likewise, no amount of arguing and articulating is going to disprove that $3 = (2 + 1)$.

So the key to this very powerful technique for personal growth and development is finding values and relationships for which the transitive property holds true. For instance, "less than" and "greater than" is a "relation" for which the transitive property does hold true. If "a" is greater than "b," and "b" is greater than "c," then "a" is greater than "c." As for the values, that's what our learning brings us to, however, I offer the following:

Throughout centuries of art, and all through the sacred writings of cultures from all over the world, the presence of the divine is indicated, again and again, by the appearance of light. In addition, we have been given specific, albeit different, names, throughout the course of history, for the divine. Names like "the Lord that healeth," and others having to do with guidance, protection and provision.

This reveals the manner by which the transitive property enables us to connect the presence of the divine to the appearance of the light to qualities such as healing, protection and provision.

Talk about the new math.

April 6, 2000

Supported by an irrational hope of the impossible

The Mulla Do-Piaza once defined "community" as "irrationals supported by hope of the impossible."

Without understanding, right away, exactly what the Mulla meant, as if he meant one thing and one thing only by it, but resonating with his definition nonetheless, I took a few moments to try and put it into other words as a way of penetrating deeper the meaning.

First of all, I considered the phrase "the impossible." Clearly, it means that which is not possible. Of course, what is and what is not possible, or at least what is *considered* possible, changes constantly. Pick any example you want. Whether it's the four-minute mile, traveling to the moon, wireless communication, pushing a button and being able to access the information in the libraries the world-over, or whatever. The point is that the determination and demarcation of what is and what is not possible is, more often than not, as history proves over and over again, an arbitrary, self-imposed limitation. To realize or achieve the impossible is to transcend our own self-limiting thoughts and behaviors. It is to become freer.

Next, I considered the word "irrationals," and decided it means the opposite of being logical and sensible. If so, then he's saying that communities are made up of people who are *not* logical and *not* sensible. Which certainly doesn't offend me any, for it seems to me that the entire *history* of greatness is filled with people who have attempted and achieved things that are not logical.

Logic is the domain of the head, not of the heart. Things

like bravery and courage and, above all, love, emanate from the heart. Perhaps he is saying that "coming from the heart," and "following your heart" reveals the pathway to impossibility.

Or perhaps he meant that the mere fact of us living together or believing in the same things, or having any common interest whatsoever is irrational, as if to suggest that we are incapable of cooperating or looking out for anyone or anything other than number one.

Maybe that's the " impossibility" we are hoping for, since, as he mentions, hope is the thing that supports us. Maybe we are all longing to not live selfishly, and to be of service to others.

"Selfishness," wrote Oscar Wilde, *"is not living as one wishes to live; it is asking others to live as one wishes to live. And unselfishness is letting other people's lives alone, not interfering with them. Selfishness always aims at creating around it an absolute uniformity of type. Unselfishness recognizes infinite variety of type as a delightful thing, accepts it, acquiesces in it, enjoys it."*

According to Wilde's definition, selfishness is an attempt to deny or limit other people's freedom, while unselfishness is letting other people be, allowing them their freedom.

The concept of limiting people's freedom versus allowing them their freedom might be subject to interpretation. For instance, the farmer who wishes to spray some sort of chemical on his crops in an effort to maximize his yield may consider legislation which makes that spraying illegal an attempt to deny or limit his freedom. On the other hand, to the person down the road wishing for clean air, clean water and untainted soil, the introduction of inorganic pollutants into the environment is, likewise, an impingement on freedom. Or, to the person with the gigantic speakers in his car, freedom might mean being able to drive around town listening to whatever music he chooses at whatever volume he chooses, while the person in the next car, or in a nearby home or building, might consider those booming sounds an encroachment on their freedom.

And maybe that's what the Mulla's saying

It's impossible to satisfy both sides. Perhaps the key is to eliminate the concept of "sides," of "us and them," and instead, see things from the perspective of just "us," the group, the world.

In order to achieve such a perspective we have to go beyond the thought of self. That is the basis of community service.

To some, that may sound irrational. To others, it may appear impossible, but to the rest of us, it is the hope that supports us.

April 10, 2000

On the matter of credit
where credit is due

Maybe it's because I've seen it a few times along the way –

A case where an incredibly creative person is found carrying on in obscurity while some other Johnny-Come-Lately pops up and starts getting acknowledged as the originator of something that the other guy was out there saying or doing years earlier – that I am sometimes suspect of how credit, in the form of public acclaim, is assigned.

For instance, anyone who has had even the most basic brush with American history has heard about the midnight ride of Paul Revere, and how he warned the people that, "The British are coming!"

We learned about the lanterns that were placed in the bell-tower window of the Old North Church, and about the signal, "one if by land and two if by sea." It is one of the principal stories of our American history, and yet who among us knows the name of the guy who placed the light in the church? I don't. Was his function, his role in kicking the revolution into high gear any less significant or risky than Paul Revere's?

And what about William Dawes? He was the other horse-riding courier that went out with Revere that night, warning people about the coming of the British troops.

While Paul Revere was heading straight to the home of Jonas Clarke in Lexington to alert John Hancock and Samuel Adams that the British were coming, and coming primarily *for them*, and in the process, letting everyone else along the road know about the coming of the British (who at the time were called "The Regulars," thus, his shouts were, "The Regulars are coming!")

Dawes, as the plan called for, was out informing a whole bunch of other people.

After Revere found the two wanted men, who were considered by the British to be the leaders of the colonial uprising, then he and Dawes set out on horseback for Concord to go and alert everyone there that the British were on their way to try and seize the colonists' supply depot. Along the way, they ran into a Doctor Prescott, who decided to join them.

Just outside the town of Lincoln, they came upon some Regulars blocking the road. With Concord waiting beyond the British barrier, the three decided to storm the blockade. Revere got captured, Dawes got away, and Prescott was the only one who actually made it on through to Concord.

So why is Paul Revere the big hero of the story?

Not that I mind. I just find it kind of curious that if you look up this story in the history books, you'll find pages and pages about Paul Revere, and barely a one-line mention of Dawes or Prescott.

I figure it's because Revere was more well-connected, and because he, like many of the primary architects of our national structure and the principles which are at its foundation, was a Mason and a member of the Knights Templar.

Another big part of the reason that we're so familiar with Revere and his ride is due to the famous poem by Longfellow that begins: *"Listen my children, and you shall hear about the midnight ride of Paul Revere."*

As far as credit goes, though, we all want to be recognized for our good work, unless our work demands that we remain incognito. Like, for instance, spy work.

And while it's great to be able to give credit where credit is due, clearly, the glory and the triumph is in the doing, in the act, the achievement, and not in the award or the reward that follows. The self-knowledge of what fears were faced and what barriers were surmounted, and too, the witnessing of the force which is capable of overcoming any and all obstacles working and expressing itself through you, is of far greater potency than the opinion of you that is held in someone else's mind. For it verifies that there does, indeed, exist such a force, and that you, just by virtue of not having gotten in its way must've done something right.

So – coaches, teachers, parents - try and instill in your kids the ecstasy of the action, the joy of accomplishment.

And if you ever find yourself feeling like you're not getting the recognition you deserve, remind yourself of the many times you didn't get blamed or criticized for things you very well could have. And then ask yourself if you're really so fired-up sure that you want your strengths and your weaknesses, your successes and your failures, your virtues and your sins made known to all.

April 18, 2000

Regarding the fossilization of the heart

Every once in a while, I'll hear a word or a phrase that really does it for me. One such example that comes immediately to mind is the term "redeployment of energy," as used by Don Juan. What it did for me, was to extend my awareness of "where" we pay attention.

For instance, say you have a teeter-totter at rest, with both ends up, parallel to the ground. Suppose, also, that you have a bunch of weights, and you want to see how many weights you can place on the teeter-totter without having it touch the ground. If you begin by placing the weights near enough to the fulcrum, which is the center bar or the point that the teeter-totter balances over, then you can place one on one side and one on the other and gradually work your way out, while still keeping the teeter-totter up in the air. It is a way of systematically extending the center outwards, but, unless the weight is very light, you have to begin, close to the center.

Applied to our own situation, each weight is a focus of attention, and depending on where we place the attention, we can either keep things "up" or send them right down to the ground.

That's just one crude yet basic way of thinking about the deployment of energy. For me, the term *redeployment of energy* helped to locate and be aware of *where* I was sending each breath.

Another term, which I just heard last night for the first time, and which set me off, is "fossilized heart."

I heard it used in a news story about a 66-million-year-old dinosaur, which was found in 1993 in South Dakota. It's a *Thescelosaurus neglectus*, so named because of the circumstances surrounding the first one of this type that was ever discovered. It happened in 1891. For whatever reason, probably because it was small in comparison to the massive sizes suggested by some of the bigger bones that were being found, no one attached much worth to it. So it was stashed away in a crate in the Smithsonian Institute, where it remained for 21 years before someone finally got an inkling to check it out, at which point, they came to find out that they had a previously undescribed type of dino on their hands.

But back to this current one, it's 13-feet long, 663 pounds, about the height of a pony, and still embedded in the hunk of stone it was discovered and excavated in.

Thanks to recently developed imaging software, the "inside" of this dinosaur can now be checked out without peeling away, and thus destroying, the outside. And what they found was a heart. A fossilized heart. That's never happened before. Up until now, the fossil record included bones and teeth and eggs, and imprints of skin or feathers or footprints. They described the heart as a "four-chambered, double-pump heart with a ... systemic aorta."

The description reminded me of a Jan & Dean song, and how they might sing about what kind of engine they got under the hood of their car.

In addition to the heart, they found tendons and cartilage and other soft tissue still attached to the bone, along the spine. A complex circulatory system, more like that of a bird or a mammal than a reptile suggests that dinosaurs, or at least this type of dinosaur, were warm-blooded creatures.

That's a claim they couldn't make even a year or so ago, because they didn't know. There was no piece of evidence they found that was conclusive one way or another.

I find that interesting, so I just thought I'd pass that much along.

But, like I said, what really struck me, right from the get-go, was the phrase "a fossilized heart."

I'd be stretching it to try and build an argument that logically implies this, so rather than involving myself in some such contrivance, I'll just flat-out say that the impression I had when I first heard and saw the phrase "fossilized heart," was that our ancestors are calling out to us, imploring us, not to let our hearts petrify and turn to stone. To keep ourselves sensitive to vibration, particularly life-vibration, for it is one of the keys necessary to unlocking our further evolution.

If you know and recognize that your heart is becoming colder and harder then know too that you are fossilizing, becoming part of the past.

Hardening of the bones and arteries is not a natural, and need not be an inevitable result of aging. Neither is hardening of the heart.

April 25, 2000

In thought, indeed, we say
a little prayer

"Human life is a constant want and ought to be a constant prayer."
　　　　　　　　　　　　　　　　　　　　　 - Samuel Osgood

I remember reading an interview several years ago with Rolling Thunder, the Native American holy man, who said something to the effect of how he was in a 24-hour-a-day constant state of prayer. It's something I've always aspired to, which compels me, from time to time, to ruminate upon the nature and the function of prayer.

Clearly, prayer is a highly personal matter, for there is no one way to pray and no one thing to pray for.

"Certain thoughts are prayers. There are moments when, whatever be the attitude of the body, the soul is on its knees."
　　　　　　　　　　　　　　　　　　　　　 - Victor Hugo

I read something recently that I found to be interesting and inspiring, and that caused me to claim further accountability for the circumstances of my life. To encapsulate, it said that we already are, whether we realize it or not, in a 24-hour-a-day state of prayer. That the sum of our expectations form a prayer that gets projected unto the world. That the thoughts we project upon situations and on people necessarily affect the outcomes and their behavior. It is, in essence, a restatement of the dictum that is the basis of virtually all esoteric teachings, namely, that "as a man thinketh so shall it be."

I know some people who would, I'm sure, dispute the idea, claiming that they have consistently held high expectations that have never or rarely been met.

I am reminded of a popular little saying that has to do with prayer and the matter of prayers being answered. It says that prayers *always* are answered, it's just that the answer might not be what we were hoping for, or what we might expect, and therefore, they, the answers, are not always easily discernible to us. The implication is that while it is all well and fine for us to make known our innermost needs and to pose our questions, it is hardly all right for us to insist on what the answer must be.

Having already stated that prayer is a personal matter, we can still *pray together* in groups, be they small or large groups.

I know this is a hot topic, what with the prayer in the classroom controversy and all, but the notion and the practice of people participating in some kind of group prayer goes beyond words and beyond people telling other people how they should believe and how they should behave. It's more a matter of finding strength in numbers and knowing that the whole is greater than the sum of its parts. It is this realization that led to the designation of a National Day of Prayer.

Granted, Rolling Thunder and the traditional Native Americans never needed any official proclamation, for group prayer is and always has been an essential component of their culture and their interrelationships with the animal, plant and mineral life around them.

But as far as the United States of America goes the First Continental Congress, back in 1775, called for the colonists to take part in days of fasting and prayer to help in the establishment of a new nation founded upon the principles of liberty and justice. Abraham Lincoln, too, while carrying the concerns of a nation divided, called for a National Day of Prayer in 1863.

As an annual event, the National Day of Prayer was established by a joint resolution of Congress in 1952, and signed into law by President Harry Truman. That law was amended in 1988 and signed by President Reagan designating that a National Day of Prayer is to be celebrated on the first Thursday of each May.

While there are some national holidays that don't mean a thing to me, and that I've never gotten around to participating in, our National Day of Prayer is not one of them.

And while I can't say for certain, it sure does seem to me that prayer and praying has undergone a resurgence lately. The most popular national magazines and TV news broadcasts have run stories on prayer, and the medical community has come out saying that prayer definitely aids in the healing process.

If, indeed, prayer can be thought of as the aggregate of our thought energy, of our conscious and unconscious expectations, as a reflection of our own conceptions, then, perhaps, we who pray participate in the national day this year by raising our expectations, of ourselves and others as a way of bringing out the best in us.

Perhaps by doing so, by consciously changing our expectations and the way we think about things and people, we can change, too, what we will see the next time we look out upon the world.

May 3, 2000

Rising from the stale habituality of two-dimensionality

I was flicking across the dial in my truck the other day, and I heard that old 60s protest song, "Eve of Destruction." There's this one verse in it that goes: *"You may take a trip for four days in space, But when you return it's the same old place."*

I'm pretty sure I've quoted those lines before, somewhere along the way, to point out that you can't turn your back on what's wrong in the world and expect it to be made right. Either that, or maybe I cited the words as a way of saying that if you haven't discovered who and what you are and what's important right here, then you're likely not going to find it there. But today, I'm finding myself on the other side of these words, having found out that, sometimes, all you need is four days to make that "same old place" seem new again, that is, to get a new, or renewed, appreciation for it.

Because even in Paradise things can turn into a habit. Even beauty can start to look plain, and even the extraordinary can become old hat.

In my case, I can honestly say that I went for days, weeks, months and even years on end, carrying around a very real and powerful feeling of gratefulness. I didn't have to work to conjure it up, it was always there. I was in a perpetual state of thankfulness that I got to live in a place I love, with a person I love, doing things for work and money that I love. But lately, when I hear myself saying how grateful I am, it's almost as if it's a reminder. It's still true, no doubt about it, and I wouldn't suggest anything to the contrary, but the feeling of it is not as close or ever-present.

It's like some of those memories of early childhood. Sometimes we're not sure whether we *really* remember doing certain things, or whether we just remember them because over the years, other people, family members mostly, have *told us* that we did those things. They remember us doing them, and sometimes their remembering becomes our remembering.

It's not that the feeling itself fades or diminishes, it just becomes familiar, and sometimes, that which is familiar fails to draw our attention.

And that's where the four days, or three days, or three months, or whatever, comes in. It's just a way of breaking up the routine. Of waking up your senses by forcing them to have to observe and take notice of some different things. It doesn't have to be anything extravagant or spectacular, it's just a matter of putting yourself in a different pace and tempo, with different scenery; different sounds and smells, and different colors.

For me, Bakersfield, of all places, did it, but it could've been anywhere. Anyplace that pulls you out of the "two-dimensionality of stale habituality."

I was lucky in that something came up which required me to be out of town for those four days just when I was reaching the point of really needing a change of scenery. However, travel is not always an option, and in those cases, we need to find ways of disrupting the routine without having to get out of town.

It becomes a matter of finding ways to keep our sense-of-wonder-and-appreciation-muscles from atrophying. We can change little things like what time we wake up, what time we work out, when we eat, what we eat, and which roads we drive down. Such simple little measures could help to wake and shake us from the sleep we get lulled into by the monotony of regular routine. I tend to think, however, that the changes in consciousness brought about in this way would be short-lived and mostly on the surface, since these things don't require any real emotional effort or investment of self. More profound changes could be brought about if we could not only shuffle around our schedule, but rearrange, too, our thinking and our acting, and the manner in which we greet each day. If we could recover our curiosity and keep in mind that we don't already know everything, that there is still a thing or two Life has to teach us.

Thus, the key is to remain reverent of Life and learning. The challenge is to stay fresh.

May 9, 2000

Bringing life into dreams and dreams into life

*"Until we dream of Life,
and Life becomes a dream."*
- Stevie Wonder,
"I'll Be Loving You Always"

I don't know if it's just the people I cross paths with or what, but I sure have been hearing a lot of people describing, in great detail I might add, dreams they've been having lately.

A couple days ago, I heard four different people, within the span of a few hours, talking about their dreams. Two of them were speaking directly to me, and two were talking with other people, and I just happened to overhear.

And that happened just a day or two after I woke up remembering the most vivid and poignant dream I've had in years. So vivid, in fact, that it didn't really seem like it was "just a dream." Instead, it felt like me and the other guy who it involved got together in another dimension and aired things out between us.

The other guy is someone I've been close with at different times in my life, although we've not spoken for five or six years due to this "thing" that's there between us. I'm not saying that because of the dream anything has been worked out between us, but we definitely made contact, and that's a start.

Energized by the ethereal exchange, I found myself thinking that in dreams is the perfect place for settling the unsettled in our lives and for casting light upon obscure situations. And it occurred to me what a potent tool it would be to know how to consciously bring things into dreams to be realized, worked out or learned from.

"Whenever I want you all I have to do is dream."

- Boudleaux Bryant

That's exactly what a major portion of Don Juan's teachings, as told by Carlos Castaneda, are about – the art of dreaming.

Dreaming, according to Don Juan, is an art in which we suspend our ordinary interpretations of things, allowing a new way of perceiving and responding to the world around us.

"To dream," said Don Juan, *"is to perceive more than we believe is possible to perceive, and to act in ways that are beyond our usual capabilities."*

He said, *"Dreaming is not learned, it's intended,"* meaning, according to Carlos, *"that it's accomplished by awakening our natural link with the vibratory force of intelligence in the universe that seers call the active side of infinity, or intent."*

I don't recall "intending" to create the scene of my dream the other day, although once I was there I did feel like I was consciously keeping myself there. Even after I stirred from my slumber, I was still able to navigate, or will myself back there, to prolong the exchange.

And while Castaneda's explanation of the role intent plays may begin to get into the abstract mechanics of dreaming, it doesn't address the issue of why I'm hearing so many people talking about their dreams lately.

I hadn't considered it before, but now that I ask myself why, a voice rises up from within, or maybe from infinity, and it suggests to me that maybe it's because the distance between the dreams of our sleep and the reality of our waking and walking is somehow becoming shorter.

I think it's just part of us becoming more aware of ourselves and our many aspects. If we can be aware, for instance, of our emotional and physical states at the same time, knowing that feelings do not exist in the bones or the blood or the nerves or the muscles, then is it not also conceivable that we can become aware of ourselves in all the various dimensions in which we exist simultaneously? If so, then perhaps we can let dreams of our better selves spill over into our waking and walking world."

"In my dreams I can see
A love that could be."
    - David Crosby
    "In My Dreams"

May 11, 2000

*Finding meaning
in the full moon of May*

Stepped outside last night, several hours after dark, and I was surprised to find that I could see my shadow just as distinctly as if it were midday. It was cold and windy, and I looked up to observe the source – well, not the source, but the agent – of the light pouring down on us through the night, an almost full moon. Not a yellow moon, or a golden moon, not a red, blue or silvery moon, but a bright white moon.

Maybe that's why they call the full moon of May the Milk Moon. Though, according to lore, the name relates to the cattle, which, by the month of May are producing plenty of milk, and not to the color or quality of the light.

A more popular name for this month's moon is the Flower Moon, which, of course, comes because of all the flowers that blossom in May.

I often turn to the moon and other celestial objects for guidance, for words or names that might help reveal the meaning of the moment, the reason of the season, the Life-rhythm of Nature. In such a way do I regard the name "The Flower Moon."

The first cue I take from the name is that now is the time for the beauty within us to burst forth and blossom that it may be seen and sensed in the world.

Clearly, that which is beautiful within us has to do with our virtue and not our appearance. And so, the ritual associated with the time of the Flower Moon is to cause our own privately-conceived virtue-buds to bloom. Perhaps this bud here is patience. That one there might be prudence, and there are those of faith, hope and charity, or whichever other ones you care to conceive and name.

Thus far, I've focused on the word "flower" only as a verb, but a consideration of the word as a noun leads to the same realizations. For if we ruminate upon the loveliness of the flower, we are forced to admit how quickly it fades. But the beauty that awakens our senses and stimulates the secret nerve in our hearts, *that* remains with us long after the petals have fallen.

The realization of that which remains, that which endures was the central focus of the life and work of Siddhartha Gautama, the Buddha. The Buddha, who lived 2,500 years ago, noted that human life is an existence of suffering caused by a desire for things that cannot possible satisfy the eternal spirit, which is no doubt the controlling agent of our existence. He said that suffering can be transcended by following what he called the Noble Eightfold Path. It is a practical method of bringing virtue buds to bloom. Buddhists the world over commemorate the Buddha's enlightenment on the night of the full moon of May. It represents the moment that his spiritual understanding shifted from the temporal to the eternal. It provides us with a further clue for the meaning of the Flower Moon. It is a reminder that now is a good time to shift our attention from that which is fleeting to that which endures.

As a final clue, for myself, I turn to the ceremony of some of my, shall we say, "old religion" friends who celebrate the May full moon as the Dyad Moon. It represents the marriage of the God and the Goddess, the male and the female, the balance of the opposites, which is exactly the same thing as the Buddha's middle path.

Whether we speak of beauty, virtue, wisdom, enlightenment or balance, it's all about that which can endure.

"Nothing but beauty and wisdom deserve immortality."

- Will Durant

May we tend to our virtue as if it were a flower in the garden, helping it to grow, as we grow in our awareness of the eternal.

May 18, 2000

Simon says, 'Judge not and feel free'

I got to thinking, recently, about some friends who aren't here anymore, meaning ones who've passed on. I thought of my dear, sensitive, art-loving friend, Simon, and I recalled him telling me, on several different occasions, how one of the most liberating things that ever happened to him was when he came to the realization that he didn't necessarily have to have an opinion about everything. He didn't have to decide if a thing was good or bad, if he liked it or if he didn't. He could, in his words, "suspend judgment."

Having reconsidered his statement from where I'm at now, I can understand why Simon might have felt freed up by doing away with judgments, because to judge is to draw a line, or, in three dimensions, to put up a wall, and then to announce, "I exist here on this side," thus, closing off everything on the other side or the other half of the universe.

Of course, if we think about it in terms of the world, which is round, and not in terms of the universe, which, as strange as it might sound, is flat, then we are reminded that if we just keep going far enough on this side we'll eventually wind up on that side. Thus, from a strictly geometrical standpoint, there are no sides, unless, maybe, we want to consider the in-side and the out-side.

By making judgments, especially about people, we construct a box or a cell, and then place the object of our judgment inside that cell. We contain it, by containing our perception of it. So, in a very real sense, we limit ourselves when we make judgments.

Unfortunately, sometimes judgments limit not only the one making the judgment, but also the one being judged. I think, here, of the parent who calls the child stupid, or who implies that the child is not strong enough, or pretty enough, or talented enough, and so, eventually what happens is that the child starts to believe it. Often, the child ends up not even trying because what's the use, they already know they're not good enough.

That's an obvious example, but there are all sorts of subtler judgments that go on all the time between people who don't even know each other, people who've had little or no interaction. The judgments are formulated on the premise of appearance, based on things like hairstyle or how the person dresses, or what kind of car he drives, or what kind of job she has. We filter all those things through the residue of our past encounters and we come up with a profile for what the person is like; what they're interested in, and how wise or unwise they must be. Having already made up our minds about them, there's no need to have to waste time getting to know them.

And then there's the matter of believing what others say. I thought I was more unbiased than that, but recently, I got to talking with this guy who had just sold his house and was preparing to move out of town. In almost no time at all, we found ourselves having a friendly and interesting conversation, and I realized, and not without some embarrassment, that, over the course of several months, I had let what someone else had said about this person get in the way.

I've been on the other side of that one too.

Which brings to mind the Sufi saying that goes, "*If you want to know what he's like - reverse what his opponents say.*"

Intellectually, we know that being judgmental is foolish, but that doesn't stop us from going around making all kind of judgments about darn near everything we see and hear. It takes effort to halt the inclination to form opinions about things, to experience and learn from Life and not judge Life.

The irony, or so it would seem, is that learning (from experience) is what equips us to judge, to evaluate, to decide whether to accept or reject things. There's certainly nothing wrong with embracing some things while ignoring others, of saying, hey, I know who and what I am and this is for me and that's not.

The difference is the same difference between what Gurdjieff called *formation* and *formulation*. *Formation* means that opinions and judgments *form* automatically without our initiating them or being able to control them, as if in a knee-jerk reaction to whatever sensory stimuli we're exposed to. *Formulation*, on the other hand, is a conscious process. If it's conscious, it suggests that we're in control of it rather than being controlled by it. And that's why I say I can understand Simon feeling liberated by not making judgments.

And while on the subject of Simon, I recall two other things he said to me, and often. One had to do with how he avoided a lot of inner turmoil by focusing on what he knew he wanted to do and not worrying about money. The other was how surprised and delighted he was to discover that he could pray for faith. Before that, he always thought that in order to pray you had to already *have* faith. But then he found out you could *get* faith by praying. But those, I suppose, are discussions best left for another time.

May 24, 2000

The topic, she said, is measurement

Sometimes, the Universe puts it right in your lap in such a blatant manner.

Take this morning, for instance. I woke up earlier than normal with the intention of getting a head start on the work.

Now, there's the work, and there's The Work. The work is what we do and how we make a living, or in some cases, how we try to make a living. The Work, on the other hand, is what we're here for – to live, to love, to learn; to learn to love to live; to evolve; to grow in our awareness of the all that is in all and the I Am that I Am.

It is, indeed, a blessing when you feel like the work is part of the Work, consistent and in the same direction.

For me, the work is writing, and this morning the question

was "what to write about?" That's what was on my mind as I began the day with a trip down to the corner store to get some milk for my coffee.

"That'll be two-nineteen," said the clerk, as I placed the carton on the counter.

"Two-nineteen?" I asked incredulously. "For a quart of milk?"

"It's a half-gallon," she said, and then she looked at me pointedly and declared, "The topic for today is measurement. Measurement of time, measurement of ..." and her words trailed off, as I realized that there it was, she had given me my assignment for the day.

Measurement is essentially a process of comparison. Comparing, for example, the length or the weight of a thing to some accepted standard, such as a foot or a pound, a gallon or a mile, a karat or and acre, a second or a degree. Obviously, it's extremely useful for us to be able to make such comparisons so that we can do things like cut wood to the right length for the house we're building, or attach a price to the quantity of food we're buying or selling, or to know how much time to give ourselves to get there.

Problems arise when we start trying to measure people, when we compare ourselves or others to some external standards.

Clearly, we can see and understand that we're all unique individuals, that no two of us are exactly the same. So how can we think or expect that our standards or desires would or could be the same? And yet, we're constantly being bombarded, like in commercials for example, with messages telling us what we should want and what will make us happy.

And while we may well get our ideas of what is worthwhile and worth having and pursuing from others, such as from parents or various other teachers, still, those ideas have to be molded and shaped by our own hands and minds and baked in the ovens of our own counsel and disposition. Or, in keeping with the idea of measurement, placed on the balance of one's heart.

To try and measure yourself according to someone else's standards is like weighing yourself on someone else's bathroom scale; you don't really know how true it is. It's like looking in one of the mirrors at the circus. The picture is always going to be a little, or in some cases a lot, distorted.

That, however, is the nature of measurement. For no matter how precise, measurement, all measurement, is still, at best, just an approximation. And who wants to be an approximation? To have any part or portion of our aspects trimmed?

A more accurate assessment and truer idea of value, called self-esteem by some, is reached by gazing, instead, into the mirror of one's soul.

Shakespeare said it when, in Hamlet, he wrote, "This above all else, to thine ownself be true."

It's a lofty creed to live by. To use it as a measuring stick, that is, to measure yourself according to your own standards, requires the development of both conscience and courage; the faculty of hearing and responding to the voice of the inner guide energized by an inner strength and resolve.

June 23, 2000

On the matter of dissolving clouds

As I merged into the left-turn lane, and was waiting for the oncoming traffic to clear, I caught myself falling into one of my old routines – dissolving clouds.

Back when we used to drive for hours, days and weeks on end, we would often pass the time dissolving clouds. We'd pick one out, and stare at it through the window of the van, and gradually we would erase it from the sky. For us, it was like doing push-ups or sit-ups, only it was using our psychic muscles instead.

I remember one time, we were accompanied on a stretch of the tour by a guy who was highly skeptical of our claim that we, or anyone, could make clouds disappear. So we went ahead and showed him. It didn't sway him, though. He was sure we had picked one out that was already thinning and dissolving, and that would have disappeared on its own without any help from us. So we let him pick the next one, and again, in a matter of minutes the cloud in question was nothing more than a fading memory. At that point, he got kind of spooked. He thought we were witches, or something.

We tried assuaging his fears by telling him that anyone can do it, it doesn't take any special powers or aptitude.

As we started to explain to him how to do it, it was revealed that none of us "did it" in the same way. It wasn't like there was a specific procedure, or a trick to it, that we all followed. So our instructions to him were to "just do it," in whatever way that he could imagine it.

He got real quiet in the back seat, I thought, mulling over what we had said. Then, after a long silence, long enough that we had already moved on to something else in our thinking, or if there was conversation, in that too, he shouted, "I did it!" He was like a little child in his excitement, and his pride in accomplishment.

So as I was waiting to make the left at the gas station, my attention was drawn to a smallish, though not puny, cloud in the sky to the north of me. And without even thinking about it, I commenced the familiar technique of erasing it starting from the outer edges and working my way in. It's like if you have a big pencil smudge on a piece of paper and you want to erase it. You don't start from the middle or the thickest part of the smudge, you start from the outside and gradually thin it out. Before I completed my turn, the cloud had been reduced in half.

I was interrupted and pulled from the process as I recalled the saying, "Through faith men can move mountains," and its adjunct that says when you reach that point you realize why move them, they're already in the right place and where they belong.

The part of me that cares to get involved with rationalization or debate might point out that there may be a practical benefit to dissolving clouds that has to do with global warming.

It's common knowledge that the amount of carbon dioxide present in the atmosphere is one of the chief factors effecting global warming, but so too is the amount of cloud cover. For clouds act as an insulation that keeps the heat in and close to the surface of the planet, thus resulting in an increase in temperature. But clouds also serve as a shield reflecting sunlight away from the planet, which suggests that they might help keep things cool down here closer to the surface. One might wonder, then, what is the net effect of cloudy skies. Do they make things hotter or keep things cooled off? One could argue that dissolving clouds, and knowing which ones to leave alone, is a means of regulating the earth's temperature, a grand heating and cooling system.

Or, as I did when I caught myself in the middle of the left-turn, you could say that removing clouds allows more light to shine.

But all of that, I know, is but rationalization. For I know that the true and practical use of dissolving clouds has nothing to do with the outer light, but the inner, divine light. It's about learning how to identify and dissolve the clouds that would block the light of the soul, and as such, it is a technique for illumination.

June 29, 2000

KISS, Kiss:
Leaving well enough alone

I have a friend whose grandfather lives up in the snow country, and has for some 60 odd years.

For as long as he's been there, he's been happily shoveling snow to clear away the driveway and sidewalks.

A few years back the grandkids decided to buy the old man, who by then had reached the ripe old age of 96, a Christmas gift that they thought would make his life a lot easier. They bought him a gasoline-powered snow blower.

So on Christmas morning, the family gathered around and got the blower ready for operation. Gramps took it outside and gave it a try, but on his first time using it, he got his hand caught in it and two fingers were cut off. Needless to say, he was like, "Couldn't we just leave well enough alone?"

I can dig it, for it seems like I'm surrounded by gadgets that are supposed to make my life easier, but which, instead, just complicate the heck out of things.

Take, for example, my garden. It's certainly no grand, award-winning horticultural achievement, but it's great in that it has the vegetables I like to eat most – tomatoes, which are really a fruit, peppers, onions and Swiss chard, as well as beans, corn and squash.

I like to go out there either in the early morning or the early evening, grab the hose and water it. It takes a little while, but it's easy on my mind.

Recently, I had a friend over visiting who told me he had a sprinkler that would be perfect for watering my garden, and he asked if I would like to have it. I thought about the 20 minutes or so a day that could be spent doing something else, so I said, "Sure, I'll take it," figuring I would pick it up one of these times when I was over at his house. Instead, he brought it over to my house the next day, just before we were getting ready to go to a party, so I put it next to my hose, and left it for later.

This morning, when I went out to water the garden, I saw the sprinkler sitting there, so I decided to put it to use.

It's not the kind that just sits there on the surface and does its thing, it's the kind you stick into the soil in a strategic spot, and you adjust the angle of spread so that the spray of water sweeps back and forth so as to drench all of the plants.

Well, even though my soil is pretty good soil, and my veggies are growing quite nicely, thank you, still, the ground was too hard for me to get this sprinkling device to stick in the dirt. There's this metal wedge sticking out the side of the spray nozzle for you to step on and drive the sprinkler into the ground, but it still wasn't going in, so I grabbed a hammer to pound it in. I hit it a few times and it started to sink into the earth, a few more times, and it went a little deeper, but still not deep enough, so one more whack and, bang, the wedge broke off.

But at least the sprinkler was standing. So I turned on the water, and checked it out. The coverage angle wasn't quite right, so I adjusted and re-adjusted, but it became apparent that I didn't have the sprinkler placed in the right spot, so I moved it.

But then, there was the matter of getting it in the ground again. With no wedge to step on or pound, I knew I had to find another way. I tapped on the top of the head lightly, knowing that it probably wasn't a good idea, but it seemed sturdy, and my taps were driving it into the ground. So I continued tapping until it was stuck far enough into the ground. But lo and behold, my tapping depressed the spring in the device so that it wouldn't spray water.

There I was, standing with my new running shoes all covered in mud, and I was thinking about, and feeling like, my friend's grandfather.

Granted, I didn't lose my fingers but these are the kinds of things that make me lose my mind.

And as I unscrewed the sprinkler head and went back to watering the garden by hand with the hose, I recalled the KISS principle, which admonishes us to "keep it simple (stupid)," and I thought about one of my brother's old songs with the chorus that goes:

"Trying to be simple
Such a very hard thing to do."

July 6, 2000

Setting sail for a new world

Just before dawn on Aug. 3, 1492, Christopher Columbus set sail for a new world. It was his intention to sail west to get to the East, because the East held great riches and exotic cultures.

Europeans had been traveling *east* to get to the East for more than 200 years, and coming back with jewels and all sorts of wonderful stuff, but that required passage over dangerous land routes. It would definitely be a big advantage for them if they could transport goods from the East on ships, so a bunch of Portuguese sea captains, since Portugal was the great sea power in those days, started looking for an eastern sea route to get to the East.

And since that gig was already taken, Columbus decided he'd go west.

People often give Columbus credit for proving that the world was round, but all the educated people of his day already knew the world was round. They just didn't know how big the Earth was. Columbus believed he could sail 3,000 miles west from Spain and arrive at China. He drew his calculations from a bunch of different sources such as the Bible, the writings of Ptolemy and Marco Polo, and Pierre d'Ailly's "Imago Mundi" (Picture of the World). He accepted the information that supported his belief and rejected everything else, which brings to mind the Paul Simon line: "*Still a man hears what he wants to hear and disregards the rest.*"

Columbus proposed his plan for a westward journey to King John of Portugal. While the king was still considering it, Bartholomew Diaz discovered an eastern route to Asia around the Cape of Good Hope, which meant that Portugal had no need for an alternate western route. So Columbus presented the plan to King Ferdinand and Queen Isabella of Spain, who eventually gave him the bread and said, "Aw, go 'head."

After two months out on the Atlantic Ocean, Columbus' men grew disillusioned, and finally, on Oct. 9, they said, "If we don't spot land in three days, we're turning back." Wouldn't you know it, three days later, they spotted land in what we now call the Bahamas.

When Columbus rowed ashore, some natives came out to meet him. Them that lived there called the place Guanahani, but Columbus said, "Uh uh, it's called San Salvador ... Not only that, *you guys* are called Indians ... Oh yeah, and from now on, *we* own the place."

And what made it even more audacious, is that Columbus *thought* he was in Asia, a place he knew full well people already lived in and had plenty of business dealings happening.

Realizing that, I guess, is why I don't celebrate Oct. 12 as Columbus Day, because I don't condone what he did once he landed, and nor do I consider it some grand and noble achievement.

But Aug. 3, that's a different story. Setting sail off into the unknown, the adventurous spirit, big dreams and bold undertakings, those are all things I can appreciate.

Lately, I've been into ceremony and ritual, even more than usual. No high falutin' kind of stuff, no subscribing to any set system, or exact definitions or specific interpretations, just a way of bringing more meaning on in. Which is why I'm celebrating today as "Set Sail for New Worlds Day."

But in this day and age, going to a new world doesn't mean finding some geographical location where no one else has been before, it's about finding a new state of mind, and thus, creating a new world for yourself. For instance, if you've been stressed out and you find a way to get rid of that stress, then, for you, that represents a new world. If money's the problem, and you find a way to make money not be a problem, whether it's by making a ton of it, or by changing your attitude about it, then that's a new world. And if you fall in love anew, even if it's with people or places or things you've loved for a long time, then that too puts you smack dab inside a world that is new.

Columbus' journey to the new world, which actually brought him to a world that was very old, in the sense that people and cultures had been existing there for more than 20,000 years, was one of the pivotal events in world history. It opened up a new world for Europeans and initiated the spread of what has been called Western civilization, though they certainly didn't act very civilized. It also helped kick into high gear a period of exploration, invention, and discovery that marked an extremely exciting time in the history of humankind and of art and science. Similarly, by creating a new mind, we can bring ourselves into new spheres, marked by exploration, invention and discovery, and likewise find ourselves in a very exciting time.

August 3, 2000

Looking to forgive? Forget about it.

There was this episode from the situation comedy television series "Taxi," which was popular in the late 1970s and early 1980s, where Alex Reiger, the intellectual, advice-giving cab driver played by Judd Hirsch, ended up going out on a date and *making nik nik* with Latka's mother. Latka was the immigrant mechanic played by the late comic genius Andy Kauffman. When Latka found out about his mother and Alex, he decided he could never speak to Reiger again. Alex tried everything to mend the friendship, but to Latka, it was a matter of honor that could not possibly be excused.

In a final appeal for forgiveness, Reiger pleaded, "Isn't there anything we can do?"

"There is one thing," replied Latka, "we could globnik."

"Globnik? What's that?" asked Reiger.

Latka was unable to explain it in English, so, instead, he handed Alex an English translation dictionary. Reiger looked up 'globnik,' and read: "**Globnik:** *To pretend like it never happened.*"

"You mean we could just pretend like it never happened?" asked Reiger.

"Like what never happened," answered Latka, indicating that the matter was over and done with.

It's a case of forgive and forget, with the emphasis on the forget part.

I think people have a tendency to think that the latter, the forgetting, can only happen after the former, the forgiving has occurred. But recently, I witnessed a couple of instances where, it seems, it was only possible to arrive at forgiveness by first forgetting.

To be in the consciousness of "I forgive you," is to maintain that, "As far as I'm concerned, you did something wrong, and even though I'm aware of it, I'm willing to overlook it." Often times, that kind of an attitude and approach only keeps the judgment of a wrongdoing and the wrongdoing itself alive.

There are some who claim that forgiving is easy, but forgetting is much harder, but as Henry Ward Beecher said: "*To say, 'I can forgive, but I cannot forget,' is only another way of saying, 'I will not forgive.'*"

Some maintain that it's dangerous to forget, if not also to

forgive, for it invites further violation upon ourselves. But that is suggestive of an unconscious type of forgetting, like when you forget where you left your keys, or an appointment you had scheduled. The kind of forgetting I'm talking about is a conscious forgetting. It's a method of stowing away the past for the sake of carrying on in the present.

It begins with a choice, and the choice is that you are willing to continue to co-exist and interact with the person who, you feel, did you wrong.

That's followed by the realization that everyone has a point of view, and that, while from your point of view things may have looked a particular way, it's likely that from the other person's point of view, it looked different.

A third step, though not necessarily THEE third step, in terms of linear order, is to give up the desire to understand and be understood. Because, inevitably, that's going to get you talking about it, which will only bring you back to the problem. All of a sudden you've got people defending what they did and why they did it, or talking about how they were hurt or disappointed by what the other person did, or didn't do. And that just leaves room for a lot of possible ways and places that things can get derailed. An extension of this realization is that not only does everyone have a point of view but everyone does what they think or what they feel is right, or best, each and every step along the way. At any given moment, if we knew the right thing to do or say, we would do and say it. It's not that we don't do it and don't say it because we don't want to, it's because we don't know any better.

With that realization, I've been able to ask myself, on the occasions when I've felt wronged, 'How can you withhold kindness and compassion from someone for being only as wise as they are?'

I doubt whether psychologists and psychiatrists and other psycho-therapists would recommend *pretending like it didn't happen* as a healthy way of getting past something that's bothering you, but it's hard to argue with results.

We're taught and reminded, over and over again, from religious, philosophical and psychological standpoints, about the virtues of forgiveness. How they are happiest the most who forgive the most, and how forgiveness is one of the sublime enjoyments of life. But we're not taught *how* to forgive, which is somewhat understandable considering that there's no one way to do it. Everybody's got to do what works for them. One technique that has been shown to work for at least some people is simply to *forget about it*.

August 8, 2000

What we do
in relation to what we are

Had someone visiting for a few days who lives in one of the desert towns along the California-Arizona border. During the time she was here, we also had a lot of other people dropping by, and invariably, whenever someone would find out where she lived, they would react with such surprise, and ask, "What do people *do* there?"

When the first person asked it, I saw my guest get, what appeared to me to be, overly defensive. I could tell it was a touchy subject, though I wasn't exactly sure why. But by the time the third or fourth had asked it, I too started getting defensive about it, and I noticed myself trying to jump in and "be there" for my guest, and let her know, without saying it, that we don't think she's odd or freakish because of where she lives.

I know that the people who were asking the question had no intention of being rude, but that's how they came across. I think they were sincerely curious, but because of the way they expressed that curiosity they made the person feel self-conscious, and thus, put that person on the defensive, which unfortunately created a division in the room or on the porch.

It's no big deal, for I think she's secure enough with herself to deal with that kind of perceived challenge, but I find it interesting that the first thing that popped into several different people's heads when they heard where she was from was to wonder "what do people do there?"

Interestingly, I was at a party the other day and there was a couple there from the town over the hill, 30 miles away - but their town is a city and my town is the country, and therein lies the difference - and they wanted to know what people here, in my town, do. And I recalled the whole thing that happened with my recent houseguest.

"I like to look at the stars," I said, in answer to their question, and a few minutes later I added that "taking walks" is something else I do.

I don't know if that's the kind of thing they were looking for, or interested in, but as these are two of the things I regularly do, and since my neighborhood is particularly well suited to doing them, I figured they were worthy of mention.

It calls to mind a couple of things.

First of all, a word - "ecocentricity" - that my boyhood friend and I would sometimes use to describe a type of awareness that's heavily reliant on place and circumstance.

It's like that map of the United States that shows LA as the whole left third of the map, New York as the right third, and all that other insignificant stuff in-between as the middle third. It's an arrogance that says there is something more valid about this way then that way. And while I certainly appreciate our differences, and the flavors and characteristics that go along with being from a particular place, still, there is a larger objective reality that extends beyond place.

Another thing this brings to mind is Siddhartha's answer when he was asked what he did, or rather, what he was capable of doing. He listed thinking, fasting, and waiting as his talents, the things he knew that he could do.

Generally, when we speak of what we do, we tend to focus on what we do to earn money, because the majority of the stuff we do, like, eating, sleeping, breathing, driving, etc., seem too trivial to mention. But even if we're talking only about the things we do to earn money, we still focus mostly on the outer skills, and neglect a lot of the inner things we do.

For instance, using discretion, subduing fear, trusting myself and the Universe, and putting one foot in front of the other - on a lot of different levels - are all things I do within the context of what I do to earn a living. Yet, that's not what I say I do, nor have I heard anyone else say that that's what I do to earn a living. The only reason I even point this out is because I consider those to be important skills I use, and just as we have and require classes such as computer programming, or drafting, or accounting, we should also offer, and I'm talking about in our public schools, classes that identify and teach life, personal-development and people skills. 'Course then, that raises the question of grades, and that's a whole other matter.

The point is, by focusing on the doing part, we run the risk of measuring and defining ourselves and others in terms of some external standards and according to outer pursuits and activities. As long as our self-worth and self-image is tied to something that exists outside of ourselves, it can always be diminished or taken away.

What you are says more about what you are than what you do does.

August 10, 2000

Using Newton to get what we want

A lot of people are focused on getting; getting what they want, getting what they need, getting what they feel they deserve. And they wonder how, and what they can do, to go about getting it.

There are tons of books out on the subject, not to mention all sorts of systems, seminars, workshops, and types of training sessions to teach you how to go about getting what you want. But this is one of those times when, rather than going through some long drawn-out explanation, I prefer a very simple model.

In this case, I turn to Newton, who gave us an answer with his Third Law of Motion, when he stated: "To every action, there is an equal and opposite reaction."

If we are to believe Newton, and why shouldn't we, considering he has been demonstrated, corroborated and authenticated time and time again, then we see that at least one possible solution to the problem of how to get, is, simply, to give ... and give and give.

The giving creates movement, a flow of energy. Movement suggests change, and isn't that what we want when we think or talk about *getting* something? We want things to be different from how they are right now. Maybe not a lot different, maybe just a little different; maybe a little more of this or a little less of that. In any case, in order for us to get something, that is, for something to come into our lives, there has to be movement, otherwise things don't change.

If we refrain from giving, another words, if we hold on to what we have, then we are resisting movement and change. In that case, we become a force that impedes the flow of energy, and inhibits the movement of things coming to us.

The Zen proverb that describes it says, "Empty your cup that it may be filled again."

That's an easy one to visualize, and it points out that unless we make room, nothing more, nothing new can be poured into our cup, into our lives; no new energy, no new beliefs, no new opportunities.

At times, it may seem that we just don't have enough to give; that maybe when we get more, we'll be able to give more. But that's because we get focused on quantity rather than on movement and the circulation of energy. Sure, there are times when we might not have money to give, or time to give, or even any energy to give, but that does not preclude us from, for instance, smiling, or waving hello, or making eye contact, or writing a letter or sharing an idea – anything to create the exchange, the circulation, the movement.

For it is movement that is the key.

Some people might point out that Newton's Laws aren't *always* true, that they break down at relativistic speeds, meaning speeds approaching the speed of light. True, but who among us has ever observed Newton's Laws of Motion being violated? In all things of earthly proportion, they hold true, and so, for the vast majority of our experiences, they are useful.

One of the things that makes the Third Law of Motion especially useful, is that it illustrates that we can bring about a desired result, which we call here a reaction, by putting forth a specific action.

It's worth pointing out here that the action, whatever it may be, is a vector, meaning that it has both magnitude and direction. When we talk about "equal and opposite," the equal has to do with the magnitude, and the opposite has to do with the direction. For instance, if we want to receive love, giving hate is not the equal and opposite of that; it is the *opposite* and opposite, and that doesn't get us anywhere. Giving love is the equal and opposite of receiving love.

Suppose what we really want to do is *give love*. What would be the action we could initiate to bring about that reaction? Two possible actions come to my mind. We know it involves love and loving, because that's the "equal" part, and again, the opposite pertains to direction. So my thought is that by loving ourselves, we make it more and more possible for ourselves to love someone (or everyone) else. Another action we could take to create the reaction of us giving love, is to perceive and acknowledge higher love, divine love, flowing unconditionally to us. The equal and opposite is then – unconditional love flowing from us.

As for Newton's Laws breaking down at relativistic speeds, the equivalent of quantum values in this discussion occurs when the act, the actor and the action - the giving, the giver and the gift – all become One.

Until then, the Third Law holds.

August 17, 2000

Highways, my ways, and days-gone-by-ways

Who among us hasn't driven across the country and said or thought, "Imagine what it was like for the settlers crossing this land."

Usually, it happens when we find ourselves coming upon some particularly arduous stretch of terrain, such as a rocky mountain, a wide muddy river, rugged bluffs or a grand canyon. In those settings, it strikes us that while *we* have smooth concrete highways to drive over, and bridges and tunnels to help us get past and beyond the obstructions, the pioneers had to haul their families and belongings in covered wagons over uneven rocky trails and through and across muddy, marshy bogs.

I remember my parents making those same comments, about the settlers and all, when I was nine years old and we were making the cross-country trek on Route 66, the classic American highway that's no longer there. It's been replaced by Interstates, and the Interstates are now being replaced by the Internet. And while the Internet certainly provides us with plenty enough information, the highways, such as Route 66, provide us with stories, tales and pictures of people and places in a way that no computer program can.

Images from that first drive and subsequent ones across Route 66 shall remain with me forever. Not only the obvious ones, like the morning sun reflecting off the Gateway Arch in St. Louis, but less celebrated ones too, like all the painted barns you used to see between St. Louis and Rolla advertising the Meramec Caverns.

In days to come, I might well forget the names of the three "royal stars," or who wrote "What a Wonderful World" for Satchmo, or the name of the river in China that flooded in 1931, killing 3.7 million people, or other such things that I've learned on the Internet, but I shall never, ever, forget the smell of those Chicago stockyards, or the sight of those cliff dwellings when you first cross into Arizona from New Mexico, or the chill in my bones as we huddled together under blankets in the truck that night in Amarillo. We may have been driving through one of our southernmost states, but it was, I think, the second coldest night I've ever spent in my life. The first was when we broke down, also on a road trip, on a desolate highway in Northern Indiana in the middle of a whiteout. We were stranded without heat or help for nearly 10 hours, and some of us, myself included, got frostbite. It was, and this is no exaggeration, a bona fide brush with death, and I got to see how I, and my compadres, handled it, and that's something you aren't going to find out on the World Wide Web.

When I think of all the things I've seen and learned driving around the highways and byways of this land, it's clear to me that the road has been my classroom, my geography lesson, my social study and my place of prayer. An essential part of my experience has come to me by traveling and rambling around on highways like US 66 and 23 and 41 and 89. Highways that have unlocked insight into our character and revealed secrets of our soul, but which, because they were too slow and inconvenient, have given way to superhighways that skirt around the towns and the cities and the people who live there. Highways with exits that spill off into drive-thru gas stations and fast food restaurants, which are often one and the same. Information highways that keep us more in touch than ever, though not necessarily touching or seeing each other.

The kind of vehicles we travel in, and the roads we travel along, have changed and no doubt will continue to change. More interesting and important, though, than the mode of transportation is the quality of the journey; what changes it takes us through along the way; whether it teaches us something about ourselves, and our fellow human beings; and about place.

While each technological advancement might cause the world to become smaller and smaller, we mustn't allow our dreams and our stories to become small, too. Or ordinary, or too much the same, for there is so much glorious diversity and so many colors that make up our makeup.

The superhighways are the fastest, and in many cases, the best roads to travel, but let us not forget to occasionally take detours into the heart and the heartland of this country, along the less traveled trails, for it is there that an America, which very possibly could wind up going the way of the covered wagons, still exists. Story-telling is one way we can keep it alive. But before we can tell the stories, we first have to experience them.

May 23, 2000

Waking to the realization that I'm in need of sleep

Ever since I first got turned on to the teachings of Gurdjieff through the writings of Ouspensky, one of my chief objectives has been to wake up. For at the core of those teachings is the contention that human beings, in what most people might call the *normal* walking around state, are, in reality, *asleep*.

Gurdjieff terms the sleeping we do in our beds at night the first state of consciousness. It is an entirely subjective state, in which we are immersed in dreams. The *reality* of the outside world is beyond our apprehension.

Then we wake up and, at first glance, we are in a different state of consciousness. In this second state of consciousness, we can move around, we can speak with other people, we can see danger, get out of its way, and so on. In other words, we're in greater control of ourselves and our surroundings, and we're more cognizant of reality. But if we consider things from the standpoint of our thoughts, we find that we're really not in control at all; that we *cannot* control the flow of our thoughts, our emotions, our imagination, or where our attention goes. Not only that, but we're still very much in a subjective state. We live in a world of "I like this," "I don't like that," "I agree with this," "I don't agree with that." Our perception of things says more about *us* and how those things affect *us* than it does about how the thing truly *is*. Objective knowledge, objective reality is beyond our grasp ... until we awaken.

Of course, the whole argument regarding sleep is longer and more involved than that, but suffice it to say that the teachings made (and still do make) so much sense to me that the focus of much of my effort and self-study over the past 30 years has been to wake up.

Until last week, when it finally, FINALLY, got through my thick head that I am to be counted among the majority of Americans in that I am affected by chronic sleep deprivation.

For a long time, the most commonly cited effect of not getting enough sleep was that it caused a marked decrease in our alertness and our ability to respond in a timely and appropriate manner. Tied to that were the findings that as few as 60,000 and as many as a quarter-million automobile accidents each year in the United States are caused by people not getting enough sleep. In addition, we've been aware that sleep deprivation often results in irritability, headaches and other stress-related conditions.

And, since I don't get headaches, and since irritability and stress are conditions that can effectively be handled through bio-feedback and self-awareness techniques, I didn't concern myself too much with how many hours of sleep I got.

That attitude was further crystallized through reading the words of Walter Russell, Buckminster Fuller and others, who convinced me that we don't need all that many hours of sleep if, instead, we learn to utilize the ever-abundant source of cosmic energy. And so, I learned how to eat this finer kind of food when, clearly, there just weren't enough hours in the day to work and play *and* sleep.

But now, there's this latest bit of research, which indicates that too little sleep causes a deficiency in human growth hormone, which, in turn, results in decreased strength and muscle mass, increased fat tissue and bulging waistlines, loss of memory, weakened immunity to infection, and other signs of aging. *And,* that it pretty much only affects men in this way. In addition, the researchers found that people deprived of sleep show signs of insulin resistance, which is an early stage in the development of diabetes. That caught my attention because in my family there is a history of diabetes.

But even all that stuff didn't *really* get me to take it seriously ... not until the last couple of weeks of burning the candle at both ends left me nothing but burned out, unable, even, to talk to the people I love the most.

And so, for the time being, at least, I have a new focus; not that I will abandon the old focus. I will still work diligently in an effort to wake up, but only if I can get some sleep.

"Sleep, however, is in general so usual and so easy a refuge that its strangeness and mystery are apt to be as little heeded as are its incalculable value and its gifts of grace."
- Walter de la Mare

August 29, 2000

As important as the first step is the next step

Oh my God, she took her first step.

She let go of the table and just went for it. Walked straight into the waiting arms of her mother, who was coaxing her on bended knee from the middle of the room.

I got so giddy, I jumped for joy, and soon after started calling family and friends, proclaiming the moment.

The first step; the starting point of the proverbial journey of a thousand miles.

From here, her world now gets a whole lot bigger, as she sets out to discover it.

I don't remember taking my first step, but I remember some of the other important steps along the way that caused my world to get bigger.

I remember, for instance, heading into the woods and doing some serious exploring. It was strange and dark, moist and mysterious, and, in my mind, dangerous. There were snakes, and poison plants, and slashed car seats, and, worst of all, bad guys who went in there to do bad things or just to hide out for a while. I knew then that I had left behind, if only for a little while, the safety of my home and yard and block and playground. On that day, I realized, I think for the first time, that peril was part of the path, sure to be popping up from time to time.

And I remember skipping Mass and exploring all those secret rooms and passageways in the convent of the cloistered nuns. It struck me, then, that the more interesting and exhilarating stuff was going on behind closed doors in secret ceremonies. My interest in the esoteric was sparked as much by that expedition, as it was by any fantastic tale I might have read in any book.

And I remember a group of us riding our bikes out of town and past the next town too. I don't know what prompted us to go beyond all preexisting boundaries that day, but we did, and we went way further than ever before. I remember how it blew our minds each time we passed another road sign whose name we recognized from long drives in the car with our parents. We laughed a little nervously, hardly believing how far away from our folks we found ourselves. We couldn't talk about it when we got home, but we knew we had attained a new degree of independence that day.

And I remember my first real date with my first real love, and how I thanked God for my hands, and for the sense of touch, and the power of sensation.

I remember wandering , hand-in-hand, all night long, with a newfound friend, through the streets of the unsafe city, ending up on a rooftop just in time to catch the sunrise. How we verbalized our dreams and aspirations, and how it ignited our souls and brought out the voice of our hearts, and served as a grand affirmation at a key moment in our growing up.

And I remember getting on the plane,
and getting on the train,
and sleeping in the rain,
and hitchhiking in Spain,
and walking 'long the Seine,
and the subways, and the snow-days,
and the doorways and alleyways,
and how each of them launched a journey, which ended up expanding my horizons; providing me with images and tales, which could only have come to me once my appetite for discov-

ery exceeded my need for safety and security;

once my trust in the universe overcame any fear of the unknown

And as I watch her now, expanding into the next dimension of locomotion, I get excited imagining what lies ahead for her. And it occurs to me that **as important as the first step is the next step, for it is the one that determines where we go from here.**

When the walls and the hours seem to be pushing in, when the world gets entirely too familiar, when what's yet to come just seems humdrum, then it's time to step out and let go of whatever you're holding on to, trusting that it'll take you somewhere new, and that even if you do fall down it won't be so bad.

September 7, 2000

There's magic in the big and the small of it

It's happened to me plenty, and I'm sure it's happened to everyone else too, where you run into someone you know in someplace different than the place you know them from, like in another state or another country, or you meet someone who knows someone else you know, and it connects the two of you who are meeting in a really interesting way, and you come away from it going, "You know, it really *is* a small world." Often, such meetings make for some truly magical moments.

One such episode that comes to mind involves a meeting I had, when I was still green and just starting out, on a train in the south of France. I was on my way from Italy, heading for Barcelona, and these three guys boarded the train. Although I venerate and celebrate America the Beautiful, these three were your typical ugly Americans in that they were loud and they gobbled up space, and rather than "blending" with other people and other places, and other customs and other cultures, they expected it all to come to them, to conform to them, to cater to them. It took about a half-second to know that while we may have been in the same place at the same time, we sure weren't on the same road together. See, I was hobo-ing it, and these three, who were even younger than I was, were feeling frugal doing Europe on a mere $175 a day! They weren't what you would call my cup of tea, as far as traveling companions go, and I'm sure I wasn't theirs, but after having struggled with my clumsy Italian for a month or so I wanted the effortlessness of shared vernacular, so I hung out with them, and they let me.

In the short time that we were together, I found out that

their threesome was actually a foursome, and that their fourth had lost his passport somewhere along the way, so they left him, having agreed to meet up again in Barcelona the following week. Right after we got off the train, we parted, not only because I couldn't afford to stay where they were staying.

I'd been hanging around town for three or four days when, while sitting in the shade of a tree with a roast chicken and a bottle of sangria, I saw this kid walk by loaded with a framed backpack and looking lost. An hour or so later, I saw him again, still looking befuddled, and walking in the opposite direction. I noticed, on the chest pocket of his T-shirt, a small "Stanford" insignia. During that train-ride into town, I picked up from the conversation that their "missing fourth," whose name was Mariscal, would be attending Stanford in the fall. So there on that Barcelona boulevard, I took a chance and called out the name. The kid turned, wondering if he'd really heard someone calling his name. I called it again, and when he nodded, I approached him, causing him to tremble. I told him that I was there to take him to his friends, and that's what I did.

That's what I mean by a small world and by magic. But sometimes, a small world, in particular, the kind caused by time and the walls closing in on you, can be made bigger. One way I do it is to go outside on a great moon or glorious star night, and gaze out into the sky. For the dark of night is deeper, further away and more profound than the light of day. When I did it last night, it brought to mind Michael On Fire's "Commanche Moon," with its lyric that begins:

"La luna bella, shines like a pearl in the sky,
Trees on the hilltop, looking like people that fly.
And the wind was so still, I could hear those coyotes breathe.
Five flaming stars floating to earth in a weave."

And later on, after my emotions had been soothed and my vision expanded, I went to one of my reference sources to find out more about this moon of September. I suspected, and rightly confirmed, that this is the one they call the Harvest Moon, that is, the full moon closest to the fall equinox. But, to my utter surprise and total delight, I found out that to the inhabitants of the Chihuahuan Desert (New Mexico, Texas, northern Mexico), this one is called the Comanche Moon! They call it that because in the late 1700s, each year right around the Harvest Moon, Comanche warriors setting out from what is now Fort Stockton, Texas, would paint their bodies, mount wild horses, and go riding into Mexico for a couple of months, during which time they would capture horses, cows and people, and take them back to their home in the north. According to the handbook of the National Park Service, they crossed the Rio Grande at present-day Lajitas and then re-crossed the river just west of, get this, Mariscal Canyon.

Small world. Big night. Good magic.

And as if that wasn't enough, when my lady walked in 'round midnight, returning from her trip, one of the first things she said was, "Guess who I ran into in the Denver airport?" It was, of course, someone we know from somewhere else.

"Small world," I replied.

But big enough, thankfully, to still hold surprises and mysteries a-plenty.

September 11, 2000

Seems everyone is busy being busy

She asked if I'd called the people down South yet.

I shook my head no, explaining how between this, that and the other, I've been not only busy but busier than ever.

She snapped at me, saying "Everyone's busy. If I hear one more person complain about how busy they are, I think I'm going to throw up."

I wasn't complaining, see, because the things I'm busy with are things I love, and I consider it great fortune and a blessing to be able to be busy with things I love. Nevertheless, especially since I've heard those exact same words come out of my mouth on other occasions, I'll give her her outburst, and agree with her insinuation that we're all jugglers trying to keep the balls in the air, and we all have to find ways of dealing with all that's on our plate.

The other thing I agree with is that, like me, pretty much everyone I run into these days is talking about how busy they are. Which raises the questions, "Are we really busier than before?" and "What are we so busy doing?"

We've got machines that get us from point to point quicker than ever before, so that we can spend more time actually "being there," rather than wasting the time en route. Of course, as any traveler knows, many of the most extraordinary experiences come in the "getting there," not the "being there." The magic, as they say, is in the journey, but more and more, it seems, the journey is being forsaken in favor of the destination.

We have all these machines and tools to do the work that we used to have to do by hand, so we can do more work in less time. And, of course, computers, at work and at home, that give us greater access to more information, with ever increasing speed, allowing us to perform our jobs with greater efficiency. But towards what end? I always took the attitude that the point of technology was to allow us more time to be with our friends and families, and do the things that we really want to do.

Is that happening? I'm not so sure. I know that before I got so busy, I regularly used to meet with a group of friends and have long talks over coffee. Stories were told and ideas were kicked around, and it was both stimulating and relaxing. Can't remember the last time we got together like that.

And, before I got so busy, I used to stretch out each and every night to relax and fortify. And I used to get a lot more reading in, and I was more diligent about my workouts. The thing is, though, as far as cutting into the time, what displaces some of those activities and pastimes is writing and being with my girls, and so, I'm a mighty happy man.

On the one hand, it reminds me of Duke Ellington's answer, when he was asked if he doesn't get tired "of doing what he's doing year in and year out?"

"You're talking from the perspective," answered the Duke, "of someone who doesn't do what he enjoys most for a living."

On the other hand, it calls to mind the story of the banker and the fisherman.

The banker was at the pier of a small coastal village when a small boat with just one fisherman docked. Inside the boat were several large yellow fin tuna. The banker complimented the fisherman on the quality of his fish and asked how long it took to catch them.

"Only a little while," replied the fisherman.

The banker then asked why he didn't stay out longer and catch more fish?

The fisherman said he had enough to support his family's needs.

The banker asked, "But what do you do with the rest of your time?"

The fisherman said, "I sleep late, fish a little, play with my children, take a nap with my wife, stroll into the village at night where I sip wine and play music with my friends. I have a full and busy life."

The banker said, "You should spend more time fishing. With the proceeds from the fishing you could buy a bigger boat. With the proceeds from the bigger boat you could buy several boats, eventually you would have a fleet of fishing boats. Instead of selling your catch to a middleman you could sell directly to the processor, eventually opening your own cannery. You could control the product, processing and distribution.

Of course, you would need to leave this small village and move to the city, where you will run your expanding enterprise."

"Then what," asked the fisherman.

"When the time is right you would announce an IPO and sell your company stock to the public and become very rich, you would make millions."

"Millions... Then what?"

The banker said, "Then you could retire, move to a small coastal fishing village where you could sleep late, fish a little, play with your kids, take naps with your wife, stroll to the village at night where you could sip wine and play music with your friends."

... May we all know what it is that we enjoy the most, may we get the opportunity to do it, and may we recognize when we are already living in the village.

September 14, 2000

We all want to change the world; perhaps we can start by changing the word

I don't think it's going too far out on a limb to say that our thoughts affect our words and our words affect our thoughts. I don't know too many people who would disagree with that statement, though many of us seem to think that it's true for the other guy but not for me.

What prompts me to say this is are the many times, in the last week alone, that I've heard the word "can't" being spoken. "I can't," ... "I can't finish," "I can't start," "I can't understand." When I hear it, whether it's someone else or myself saying it, I cringe, because it feels and sounds to me like a very real barrier that we're placing upon ourselves.

Another one is the word "hate." "I hate my job," "I hate this food," "I hate that band," "I hate it when people do this, that or the other." I'm not talking about hate being expressed in the degree of, say, a hate crime, I'm talking about seemingly innocuous statements about things that might not even seem all that important.

And that's the thing, people don't think it's that big of a deal if they tell themselves, and others, that they hate something. "It's just a figure of speech," say some. "It doesn't mean anything. There aren't really those kinds of feelings behind it." But if we accept that words do, or can, have an affect on our thoughts, then is it not reasonable to think that if we are speaking such words then just maybe we're harboring or constructing beliefs and attitudes?

We understand the mechanism by which this happens, and

the likelihood of it happening, but we let it go. It's a matter of neglect.

It reminds me of Ben Franklin's story about the little horseshoe nail.

"*A little neglect,*" commented Franklin, "*may breed great mischief; for want of a nail the shoe was lost; for want of a shoe the horse was lost, and for want of a horse the rider was lost, being overtaken and slain by an enemy, all for the want of a little horseshoe nail.*"

I think the whole issue of words and negative talk and the impact it has on our situation and our self-image is much more serious than many people might suppose, and I think it warrants some attention.

In recent years, we've given a lot of attention to things like, alcohol, drugs, cigarettes, weapons and violence on account of the harm they bring to us ... to our children, our families and our communities. Words, too, I contend, can be mighty harmful; to others, yes, but even more importantly, to ourselves. For our minds believe what we tell them, and if not, well then that presents a dilemma of another sort.

Some people might think that I'm going overboard here, making a mountain out of a molehill, but is it not written that "in the beginning was the word?" I think that tells us something about the act and the process of creation, now as well as then.

Words followed by circumstances; words as self-fulfilling prophecies.

If you think it's really not that big a deal, then try controlling it and see what happens. Try not saying "can't," or "hate," or whatever other negative, limiting word occurs to you for a whole month.

I realize, of course, the futility of the admonishment; that asking a person to note or control the words that come out of his or her mouth implies that that person can remember to do so, and is aware of the words that he or she speaks. There's the contradiction, because many of the people who are engaging in negative talk are not aware of it, at least not while it's happening. But the more times we try and pay attention to it, the more times we remind ourselves to do so, then the more times we'll catch ourselves, and from there, the momentum can build.

For anyone interested in trying it, it may help to write the word "words" on a piece of paper, and keep it someplace, or several places, where you'll see it - like on the refrigerator, on the mirror, on the dashboard of your automobile.

As John Lennon noted: *"We all want to change the world."* Perhaps we can start by changing the word.

September 28, 2000

The rope, the river, and the rescue

The act of holding on
and the process of letting go

With the television news often looking like an action-adventure film, and with action-adventure films flooding the theaters and cable movie channels, it's likely most of us have seen an incident involving some sort of daring and dramatic rescue. Like, for instance, where a helicopter drops down and lowers a hi-tech rope to someone who's battling the current of a raging river. And how, once the party in peril grabs hold of the lifeline, the helicopter pulls them out of danger and carries them to safety.

Well, every now and again, I find myself feeling like the guy dangling on the rope. And in those times, despite the inner and outer voices that whisper and sometimes scream that I must DO something big about it, it seems that, instead, all I really have to do is just hold on to the lifeline and let all the craziness, and all the rushing and raging, just pass right on by beneath me until things are calm again.

Which, since I'm obviously speaking in metaphorical terms and not talking literally about an actual helicopter, raises the question of what is it that our lifeline is attached to? And answering my own question, I say that the lifeline we cling to when our circumstances are most dire is attached to what we deem to be "the important stuff." Things, I suppose, without presuming to say what is or should be important to somebody else, like faith, family and friendship.

And while I certainly cling to these things myself, the helicopter that came and dropped me a line this past week, arrived in the form of a song; in words and music.

I need not necessarily say which artist or which music did it for me, it matters only that for three days, I listened over and over again to, what to my listening ears were 10 new songs; songs which, by the beauty of their melodies, the language of the lyrics, the elegance of the arrangements, the brilliance of the background vocals and the expressiveness of the singer's phrasing, managed to yank me from the mud and muck of the mundane, and catapult me into a world of timeless abstraction. In other words, I was healed.

For such is the power of music.

And such was the rescue.

It occurs to me, as I play with the image of the rope and the river and the helicopter and the survivor, that, in one sense, the act of holding on could be considered an attempt at or a striving for security. But as Helen Keller so adequately noted, *"Security is mostly a superstition. It does not exist in nature, nor do the children of men as a whole experience it. Avoiding danger is no safer in the long run than outright exposure. Life is either a daring adventure, or nothing. Serious harm, I am afraid, has been wrought to our generation by fostering the idea that they would live secure in a permanent order of things. They have expected stability and find none within themselves or in their universe. Before it is too late they must learn and teach others that only by brave acceptance of change and all-time crisis-ethics can they rise to the height of superlative responsibility."*

There is no real security to be had as long as the thing that is being held on to is of the material world.

Which brings up yet another of the great paradoxes — that deliverance from the woes of the day is arrived at by the act of holding on and the process of letting go occurring in simultaneous fashion. Holding on to that which is eternal, and letting go of that which is temporal.

Returning, once again, to the image of the rope and the helicopter — if we let go, we plunge back into the river, which then carries us away. But if what we have let go of, is material, temporal and finite, then where, but on into the ever-changing waters of the eternal present, the timeless now, can the current carry us?

In the language of Don Juan, it is "the journey into infinity." Helen Keller calls it "the rise to the superlative of responsibility." Regardless of which description we use or which one we favor, whether we call it rescue or redemption, liberation or The Great Escape, it would seem that it is achieved by holding on to something and letting go of something else.

> *"Hold on, John*
> *John, hold on*
> *It's gonna be alright."*
> - from "Hold On"
> By John Lennon

> *"I feel like letting go."*
> - from "Letting Go"
> By Paul McCartney

October 17, 2000

Changing,
but according to unchanging laws

The mornings have been downright cold; the nights cool and crisp, clear and cloudless. Another page, another month, about to be flipped over on the wall-calendar.

Though, I don't need a measuring device to verify the changing days.

I need only step outside and walk around, and the colors, textures and temperature too, transport me to another time. Or rather, to another place at the same time, meaning, the same time of year.

Where morning is familiar and similar are the sensations. And the stars I behold *now* in the skies on *this* night are the same ones the season showed me then.

It serves as a great reminder that we are all traveling, all of us, in circles. Our position changes each and every day. To try to resist that change is to oppose the Universe. Then again, there are changes, and there are changes. And there are those things that don't change.

Which leads me to something I've been thinking about a whole bunch lately, and that is, the quality of endurance; that which has the capacity to endure.

A long time ago, a fortune-teller said to me that something in this life must endure, and that that thing is the ability to care about the world. These past few weeks, I've been substituting other words for caring; words like love, compassion, forgiveness and many others, in an effort to assemble a bigger body of , and give greater meaning to, "that which can endure." The why and the wherefore being that, in these days when we are so rushed, so busy and so filled up, it seems that the wisest and most worth-while place we could possibly place our attention, expend our energy or focus our commitment, effort and aspiration is on "that which can endure," if there is any such thing.

So, when I ponder the stars and planets whirling through space, or the seasons of nature moving through time, it brings to mind that – ever-changing is the Universe, but according to unchanging laws.

Laws that direct Winter to follow Autumn, and Spring and Summer to proceed after that; or the Earth to return to the same place relative to the sun every 365 days; or the tides to rise and fall, the birds to come and go.

No one could accuse the stars in heaven of being slaves, and yet they are utterly and unerringly bound. Unlike us; we who are unpredictable, and subject to so many laws of chance and cir-cumstance.

It may sound ironic, but the matter of our own progression and independence consists in attaching ourselves more and more fully to fewer and fewer laws. For instance, a person whose ac-tions and reactions are based on what others think or say is sub-ject to many more forces and possible causes than someone who is somewhat more self-determining. Likewise, a person who lives by a literal interpretation of the law "an eye for an eye, a tooth for a tooth" is sure to be far more erratic than someone who lives by the law "do unto others as you would have them do unto you," for there is, likely, much less variance as far as what you would want to have done to you.

To roll with the punches and flow through the changes, and to change ourselves while remaining true to our inner dictates is not only a mark of endurance but strength and flexibility as well.

In morning and at night, Nature's song sings to me to be like the seasons, and like the stars and planets; to change with the times, but to remain firm according to the inner laws that direct my aspiration.

October 26, 2000

Greater emotional reward in having tried and faltered

An image came to my mind – three guys trying to lift something heavy. It could be two guys, it could be four, it doesn't matter. Nor does it matter what they're lifting or why they're lifting it. All that matters is that it takes all of them working together to get it off the ground.

But one of them doesn't think they can do it.

"No way," he says. "There's no way we'll be able to lift that."

Undeterred, his buddies urge him to at least give it a try.

So all three of them get set and grab hold, but when it gets time to heave the ho, only two of them give it their all. The third one, the one who's sure they can't do it, doesn't fully exert himself, and doesn't really go for it. Then, when they fail to lift the load, he looks at the others and says, "See, I told you so."

His refusal to try in earnest denied them all the sense of triumph that goes with accomplishing something, especially something that you're not sure is within your grasp or capabilities. And even if they could lift it, there's still greater emotional reward in having tried and faltered than never having tried at all. But to not know what might have been because the effort was not put forth, well, there's not much to exult in there.

How many times have you, too, tried getting something off the ground, not necessarily an object, but maybe a vision or an idea, only to have someone start spouting off all the reasons why you can't do it, or why it won't work? And, as if to rationalize the resistance they're putting up, they say, "I'm just playing devil's advocate, here."

By saying that, and by adopting that stance, people might think they're being smart, or realistic, or that they're forcing you to consider something you may not have thought of before, but ... well, to quote Marvin Gaye, "*It makes me wanna holler, throw up both my hands.*"

The word "advocate," when used as a noun, as it is here, means "one who supports or urges;" "a proponent;" or, "one who pleads the case of another." So what the person claiming to play the devil's advocate is actually saying is: "I'm just supporting the devil, here," or, "I'm just being a proponent of the devil, here," or, "I'm just pleading the case of the devil, here."

Why? Why plead the devil's case? I'd much rather hang with the angels who are trying to help us find some kind of heaven on earth then some cynic who but turns each day into a living hell.

In my view, the devil is not some character with horns and a pointed tail, but rather, that force or tendency which would attempt to discourage us; to weaken our resolve, to rob us of our passion, to temper our enthusiasm, to undermine our faith, to deaden our senses our diminish our love.

Being smart is one thing, but caution, and an inordinate desire to avoid life's pratfalls, while it may spare you from a sticky wicket or two, does not, and cannot, put a twinkle in your eye, a sparkle in your cheeks, a bounce in your step or a song in your heart.

As for those who would withhold their strength and power and love, denying us all of something great and exciting, I would remind you that playing not to lose does not a winner make ... and the joy is in the doing and the being.

"The less you can enjoy, the poorer and scantier yourself; the more you can enjoy, the richer and more vigorous."
- Johann Kaspar Lavatar

"Persons extremely reserved are like old enamelled watches, which had painted covers that hindered your seeing what o'clock it was."
- Horace Walpole

November 15, 2000

Playing dot to dot on the road from Joy-zie to Betelgeuse

I got these cousins who live in Joy-zie, which is how one of my greaseball friends pronounces it.

The time spent with these folks has provided plenty of material for my tall-tale-tellin'.

Like the time she and I were driving around and we got a flat tire, and she had a jack but no spare, and so she went and jacked up someone else's car and stole the whole doggone wheel. Or the time he and I found ourselves sitting there with Bill Graham, watching some lunatic nearly knocking over the cops as he ran chasing after a ball of contraband through the streets of Soho. Not to mention the time they held the inspector upside down by his ankles over the side of the building.

New Jersey - the license plates call it The Garden State, but many people still refer to it as "the armpit of the nation."

I can think of a lot worse body parts to be called, but still, it's an insult. Though, I guess, it's only an insult if you feel insulted by it.

Anyway, it's all relative. In the grand scheme of things, it's really a very minor quip, given that the nation is but a small portion of a single planet, which is but one of gazillions and gazillions of planets, orbiting around trillions and trillions of stars.

It would be a bigger insult, I suppose, to be called the armpit of the world, or the solar system, or bigger still, of an entire constellation. That's precisely what Betelgeuse is.

I think of it because it is part of the same constellation as the three compelling stars that have my attention on this wonderful winter night. The three, known collectively as "Orion's belt," are, from west to east, Mintaka, Alnilam, and Alnitak. Betelgeuse lies approximately 10 degrees north of the belt.

To us on Earth, Betelgeuse is the 11th brightest star, though only the second brightest star in Orion. The brightest in the constellation is Rigel, which is the seventh brightest star in our sky.

The word "Betelgeuse," which comes from Bed Elgeuse, which comes from Yed Elgeuse, is Arabic, meaning "armpit of the giant;" the giant being "the hunter," the hunter being the constellation of Orion.

In Greek mythology, Orion was the "dweller of the mountain," and was famous for his prowess both as a hunter and a lover.

According to one of the stories, just one, mind you, for there are many versions and accounts, Apollo, the god of beauty, poetry, music, prophecy and healing, overheard Orion boasting one day about his skills. Convinced that Orion was bird-dogging after his sister, Artemis, Apollo went and told the Earth Goddess that this slap-happy hunter was planning on wiping out all the animals of the Earth. So the Earth Goddess sent a scorpion to go sting Orion. But being the great hunter that he was, Orion was able to fend off the venomous creature long enough to make it to the sea, and jump in and start swimming away.

Well, Apollo watched the whole thing go down, and so he went and got Artemis, who was an excellent shot, and he challenged her to see if she could hit the small target moving through the water. He told her that it was a notorious villain making a getaway. Artemis reared back her bow and let fly her arrow, and danged if she didn't nail the scoundrel on her first try. When she went out to retrieve the corpse, she found that it was Orion.

Artemis begged Zeus to restore Orion to life, but Zeus refused, so Artemis took Orion's image, and placed it in the sky, where we still see him today; the master of the winter skies, lording over the heavens from late fall to early spring, with his hunting dog Sirius trailing at his feet.

And speaking of Sirius ... in the 1930s, these two French priests reported that the Dogon tribe of Mali, West Africa, believed there was an invisible companion star to Sirius, which is smaller and much denser than its visible sibling. The question, to us who now know that there is, indeed, a dense invisible companion, becomes — how does this primitive tribe with no telescopes or astronomical instrumentation know about an invisible star?

The Dogon, according to the priests, also spoke of a third, much dimmer still, star, also connected to Sirius. In the 1990s, that third star was verified.

So how do and how did they know about it? According to them, the Nommos told them. The Nommos, they say, are a race of amphibian-looking beings who visited the Earth thousands of years ago. The Nommos, whose home planet is said to orbit around Sirius-c, also told them about Jupiter's moons and Saturn's rings, and explained to them that we and these other planets orbit around the sun.

The renowned late astronomer, Carl Sagan, explained the Dogon's knowledge of these things by saying, they must have been taught by late-19th and early-20th Century missionaries, and that their telling of these things is really just a re-telling. But that doesn't explain why the doggone Dogon have 400-year-old artifacts depicting the Sirius system, and 700-year-old ceremonies celebrating the dog-star and its companions.

... Or why the positioning and structure of the Egyptian

pyramids relates to the position of the stars in Orion.

And if that's all sounding rather mysterious, well, guess what, it is. And that's the point, for I have found that whenever I start to feel things getting dull, all I need do is look up, and embrace the mystery. Either that, or recall and relate some of the strange stories about my cousins in Joy-zie.

"The most beautiful experience we can have is the mysterious. It is the fundamental emotion which stands at the cradle of true art and true science."

– Albert Einstein

December 7, 2000

'Do you believe in ghosts?' she asked

I walked into the restaurant to pick up my take-out order, when I spotted a couple of couples I know seated at one of the tables. Seeing me standing there, waiting for my food, one of the women called out to me, asking me if I believe in ghosts. Without any hesitation, I nodded my head yes.

When she said, "We're here sharing some of our favorite ghost stories," it sounded to me like an invitation, or rather, a solicitation, for me to add a word or two about *why* I believe in ghosts. I walked over to their table and told them about the time that I witnessed my brother recording a song, by himself, in his home studio. The two of us were the only ones in the house.

After finishing the take, he pushed the playback button, and both of us were completely amazed to hear two voices singing on the tape. There was the part my brother sang, and a much fainter, though definitely discernible, high harmony part over that. No question about it, there were two voices on that tape.

As another example, I related the time that my friend took a picture of her sister through the window, and how, when the film was developed and printed, it revealed, very clearly, a second face floating just above and to the left of her sister's face.

I felt like the people sitting there at the table appreciated the matter-of-fact-ness of my simple tales; that they weren't some elaborate horror stories.

Not to deny those sorts of episodes, it's just that I don't need the horror of Amityville or the spectacle of "Poltergeists" to convince me that there are entities, presences, energies, or whatever you want to call them, that exist beyond the realm of logical explanation. Or that logical explanation often reduces unexplainable mysteries to easily and adequately accounted-for everyday occurrences.

As a kid, I had one of those typical kid episodes where my two cousins and I worked ourselves up into a frenzy, convinced that the tree branch silhouetted through the pulled-down window-shade of their upstairs bedroom was some kind of boogeyman. Their parents showed us that it was a branch, and told us that there are no such things as ghosts. But even then, I was aware of the contradiction of them saying, "there are no ghosts," and us, them included, dipping our hands in water, crossing our-selves and saying, "The Father, the Son and the Holy Ghost." Were we supposed to believe in this Ghost over here but not those ghosts over there? I quickly became more comfortable with the term "holy spirit." Though I continued to be plenty comfortable thinking and talking about ghosts.

I find it interesting that, in our effort to teach children not to be afraid, especially of the dark, we put forth all this effort and all these explanations to assure the young ones that there are no such thing as ghosts, all the while, ourselves believing that there really are ghosts. Not that everyone believes it, but a good many, if not most of us, do.

Even if we don't know, or can't say, exactly what a ghost is.

My dictionary defines "ghost" as "the spirit or soul of a dead person making itself known to the living." That would, or at least could, explain the voice on the tape and the face in the photo. Or the ripple that reaches me in the interwoven threads of the afternoon rays, which feels a whole lot like my grand-mother, who crossed over a number of years ago. Or the musi-cian who reports being inspired by the ghost of Buddy Holly, or the athlete motivated by the ghost of Jim Thorpe.

Perhaps one of the differences between our acceptance of, and belief in, ghosts today, and the ghost cults of old, has to do with us not being quite so filled with anxiety about being the recipients of mysterious bad luck. Or maybe it has to do with us not being as afraid of the dead as they used to be. Or maybe it's because we can conceive of spirits and presences that not only have supernatural powers, but supernatural intelligence as well.

So there it is. After having placed our faith in science, and having gone through the Enlightenment and the Age of Rea-son, and the Industrial Revolution, and the race for space, and the information explosion, and all the rest, here we are, again, believing in ghosts.

One other point to consider, maybe it's not other people's ghosts that we have to learn to deal with, but our own.

December 19, 2000

Remembering the Eric Canal

"I got a gal her name is Sal
Fifteen miles on the Erie Canal."

Whenever I hear or read about the Erie Canal, I automatically hear Tennessee Ernie Ford's singing voice. I don't know, maybe it is a strange connection between 16 tons and 15 miles. But when I actually stop for a minute and think about it, what comes to mind is all the digging that went on. Not the digging to connect Lake Erie with the Hudson River and the Atlantic Ocean, but the digging that went all the way from the creek to the blacktop on our old school playground.

One day, as if out of nowhere, Pierson got the notion to start gouging out a canal, just with his hands and with rocks. He was always kind of a weird guy anyway, so no one paid it much attention.

He was the biggest kid in the class, not just tall, but big. He played the tuba. I remember him carrying that thing back and forth to school. It looked like such drudgery, especially in winter. It matched his personality, though. Deep and honkin,' and slow moving. The way he walked and stuff kinda reminded me of Frankenstein. He looked old, even when we were young boys.

Despite his size, he never did much along the lines of any physical activity, other than carry that tuba. He was smart, though, especially in math.

So when we finally did take notice, and realized that he'd been out there, recess after recess, lunch period after lunch period, day after day, well, we had to start wondering just what was going on.

He was a kid with a vision, that's for sure, and when he told us of his plan to take it the whole way down, past the swings and the slide and the monkey bars, all the way to the tether-ball poles, and also to extend it up past the baseball diamond and the backstop, all the way to the creek, well, we couldn't help but cheer on his efforts. It was an enormous undertaking, and for a couple weeks, it became the talk of the playground, and even in the classroom. Eventually, we put our baseball or football or basketball game, depending on which season it was, on hold for a while, and we all joined in. Not only did we lend a hand, but we, at least temporarily, made him the boss. We told him to tell us what to do, and he did, and we did it. By this time, people were using spoons and cups and glasses and rulers, and other crude gouging tools.

I seem to recall the teacher being impressed by the way that all these different circles and groups of friends, both male and female, came together and formed a collective will around a common purpose.

He would give us our instructions, and then he would go and attend to the endpoint, which was a mini-reservoir conceived by him.

Slowly, and then not so slowly, the narrow winding trench lengthened. When it was clear that the rain was coming, we all upped our effort, knowing that we had to connect the ditch to where the reservoir was going to be if we wanted to see the water flow and the vision come alive. And none worked harder than him.

When the time came, it all worked just like it was supposed to. We stood with pride as we watched the water drain down to the low area near the basketball court. Pierson dubbed it Lake Wendelken, in honor of our teacher, 'cuz she was pretty and she was cool. But the real honor belonged to him, and so we named the ditch through which the water flowed, "the Eric Canal," for that was his first name.

And some of us even sang the song.

"...*A good ol' worker, and a good ol' pal,*
Fifteen miles on the Erie Canal"

We went all through elementary school, junior high and high school together. I never once hung out with him, except during the building of the canal.

I ran into him a few years ago, and learned that he was working in New York, the head of the Janitors' Union. And I knew, as soon as I heard it, that it was right, and that he was bringing the same kind of integrity to the halls of those schools that he brought to the playground of ours.

The Erie Canal isn't there anymore. It stopped being used more than a hundred years ago, having been replaced by the railroad, and then the railroad was replaced by the highway. But the stories that sprung from it and that passed through it, like the train tales too, still remain, and not just in books either, but somewhere deep in the fabric from which our character is woven.

The Eric Canal, too, is but a memory, but one I shall never forget, for it represents an attempt at greatness. For a brief while, it managed to pull an otherwise ordinary setting out of the realm of the flat and the dull and transform it into something wondrous, something people talked about and looked forward to. It drew people together, ignited hearts and vision, and helped create a bond between people. I'd say, anyone or anything that can do that deserves to be remembered.

"And you always know your neighbor,
you'll always know your pal,
If you ever navigated on the Erie Canal."

December 26, 2000

Let me stop thinking
so I can use my mind

Oh, the number of times these past few days I've heard myself say, "If I think about it, I'll get angry," so I try not to think about it, and instead, just continue on.

It's the old bit about mind over matter, where if you don't mind then it doesn't matter.

But just because I'm trying to keep my thoughts in check doesn't mean my mind's not astir through much of the day and most of the night. And I'd like to use it more than I do, but I keep getting distracted, having to think about things.

It's ironic that the thing that's keeping me from using my mind more is thinking.

It is a double-edge sword, this mental process we call thinking. At times, it is the agent of our release, while at other times, it is the basis of our confinement. It can get us through, it can trip us up.

It has its time and its place, that's for sure.

I think of the athlete, learning his or her assignment at practice; having to think about what they are supposed to do, or what they are going to do in a given situation. When the moment is at hand, though, in the game, or the match or the meet or the contest, there's often no time for thinking. As the speed of thought is slower than the speed of instinct or reaction, he or she that has to think is already beaten, as in beaten to the punch or the point of contact.

Or I think about the putter or the free-throw shooter, who has to control thoughts, so as to not be distracted, but cannot really be *in* thoughts, or else he or she is likely to pull it or push it or come up short or bang it too hard.

It's a fine line, knowing when and how much to think.

Those who study such things have identified different "types" of thinking, which they label "left-brain thinking" and "right-brain thinking." The left brain variety is analytical. That is, it specializes in separating things into parts, or in other words, disintegrating things, which is helpful when you're trying to figure out how to spell a long word, or divide one number by another, or devise the most efficient way of propelling a block of wood across a pond using only a balloon and a ballpoint pen. Right-brain thinking, on the other hand, is integrative. It puts things together into whole patterns, which is better for all abstract, spatial, nonlinear functions. If we're trying to become "whole," that is, to integrate body, mind and spirit, it makes sense, does it not, to employ the integrative, or right-brain, form of thinking.

Funny that a consideration of mind has led to a discussion of the brain. Funny, but not unusual, for people often tend to equate mind with brain.

Philosophers have long asked the question, "where is the mind," the real question being is the mind in the brain? It's like asking if the Mississippi River is in Mississippi. It is, but that's not the only place it is.

Rather than asking *where* the mind is, I like to ruminate upon what the mind is, and what the mind does and how the mind does it. One of the things that rings true for me, is that the mind is a great connective device, which provides at least one answer for *what* it is. As for *what it does*, my answer is that it connects, or can connect, the brain to the soul, the human to the divine, the tangible to the intangible, the finite to the infinite, the temporal to the eternal. As for how it does it, I'm thinking (and here I go thinking again) that it has to do with "intent."

One of the keys when working with intention is to not get bogged down with all the stuff in between here and there. To not have to see and trace the movements that may occur each and every step along the way, and to not have to understand all parts of the process. Rather, to simply envision, in some simultaneous fashion, "this" joining with "that," "here" extending to "there," so that there is no here or there or this or that, only a picture of your creation, and a field occupied by your presence and awareness.

It's like a big "pin the tail on the donkey" game, where you're the tail, or you're the donkey, or, whichever, it matters not, as long as the two are connected together.

And that is the function, or a function, of the mind.

... We could also talk about the obliteration of boundary...

... Ah, never mind.

January 25, 2001

A little help from my friends –
Don Juan and St. Francis

On his album "Wavelengths," Van Morrison sings *"Take it where you find it ..."* Well, today, as on so many other days, I find it in the words of Don Juan, as transcribed by Carlos Castaneda.

See, I was feeling so annoyed, enraged even, by what I perceived to be nothing less than abject tyranny. And I didn't know what to with it or do about it.

The American Way of dealing with it would be to just rebel.

"Rebellion to tyrants," wrote Benjamin Franklin, *"is obedience to God."*

And then there's the Declaration of Independence, the purpose of which was "to submit the facts to a candid world" to show that "the King of England had established a tyranny" over the colonies, and to pronounce that "a tyrant is unfit to be the ruler of a free people."

To act with the courage and the wisdom of our forefathers, then, would be to rebel. But, to tell the truth, I really didn't see what good that would do. I didn't see what I, or anyone else for that matter, stood to gain from it.

Then I remembered what Don Juan had to say about tyranny and tyrants.

"A petty tyrant," he explained, *"is a tormentor. Someone who either holds power over warriors or simply annoys them to distraction."*

He noted that, *"nothing can temper the spirit of a warrior as much as the challenge of having to deal with impossible people in positions of power."* And he pointed out that, *"The perfect ingredient for the making of a superb seer is a petty tyrant with unlimited prerogative."*

And, let me tell you, it turned the whole thing around for me. Suddenly, rather than feeling like the victim of circumstance, I found myself feeling like a very lucky boy, indeed, that my situation offered me this incredible opportunity for growth and development.

Talk about useful ...

I could, perhaps, question the usefulness of having studied and learned things like Bernoulli's equations, or Fourier transforms, or L'Hospital's rule, but there can be no doubt whatsoever of the value (for me) of having read Castaneda.

Like I said, you take it where you find it.

I could probably have just as easily cooled my jets by reciting "The Prayer of St. Francis," in particular, the part that goes, "May we seek not so much to be understood as to understand." And a lot of times I do say it, and I do embrace it, and it helps, and it gives me comfort and direction. But on this day, it was Don Juan that did it for me, and his reminder that, *"What usually exhausts us in a situation like this is the wear and tear on our self-importance. Any man who has one iota of pride is ripped apart by being made to feel worthless."*

And that's all I needed to transform the emotions. And from that moment, rather than puffing myself up, and feeling like I had to defend myself, or set the record straight, I decided, instead, to not take it, or myself, seriously; to not react, to not feel sorry, or mad, or diminished in any way. Rather, to remind myself of the forces that are protecting me and pushing me along the path of my soul, and to be grateful for that. And I am.

And I'm thanking my guardian angel,
and thanking my friends — Don Juan and St. Francis,
and thanking my teensy-weensy petty tyrant,
el pinche tiranito chiquitito.

January 30, 2001

Knowing who's where
and what moves around what

In the Third Century B.C., the Greek astronomer Aristarchus proposed the idea that the earth revolves around the sun. But the idea was rejected.

It's not hard to understand why considering that it didn't *feel* like we were moving, and because you could *see* the sun move, as it rose in the east and set in the west. So people believed that the sun revolves around the earth, rather than vice versa.

And they kept on believing that way for another 1,700 years or so, which is when the Polish astronomer Copernicus proposed his heliocentric theory, which said that the earth rotates around its axis every day, and that it also revolves around the sun every year. But, except for a small handful of scholars, most people still couldn't cope with the idea of a moving earth, so they clung to a geocentric, or earth-centered view of the solar system.

Then Galileo came along, and thanks to his superior telescope, was able to observe all kinds of stuff, like sun spots, the phases of Venus, and the moons of Jupiter, which provided direct evidence for Copernicus's theory. So Galileo became one of the most vocal supporters of the heliocentric theory, which made for some head-on collisions with the Catholic Church. As a result, Galileo was tried at an ecclesiastical court, convicted as a heretic, and sentenced to life in prison, which, after a short period, was reduced to house arrest for the remainder of his life.

Today, of course, most of us know and are taught from a young age that the earth and all the planets in our solar system revolve around the sun. But even though we know it and understand it intellectually, it still hasn't taken hold in our consciousness and in our day-to-day way of thinking. What I mean is that we still have a tendency to think and act like we're the center of things, and that everything revolves around us. It's called being egocentric, or in other words, viewing everything in relation to ones' self.

Again, it's not hard to understand why we might think this way considering that the vast majority of us perceive things from wherever we are and according to our particular circumstances. For instance, someone living in an inner city neighborhood might say that taking a walk at night is a dangerous thing to do. On the other hand, someone who lives out in the country might consider it totally safe to go walking around at night. Both are egocentric points of view based on personal experience.

Another form of egocentricity is thinking about "how is it going to affect me?" Which, again, is understandable because if *we* don't think about it and attend to it, then who is.

The danger, though, arises when egocentric thinking tends to reinforce a sense of separateness, or when it prompts us to look out only for number one. Such thinking and such behavior, like the Ptolemaic and Aristotelian views of the solar system, worked for a while, and even led to some incredible technological advancements and individual achievements. Ultimately, though, egocentric thinking, like the geocentric views of the solar system, does not reveal the truth of who and what we are, or of our place in the universe. And just like the geocentric theories eventually gave way to the heliocentric theory, likewise, the truth of our inter-connectedness will eventually replace the illusion of the separate self.

This is not to suggest that the state, the group, the company or any other organization is to be regarded as more important than the individual and his or her rights. Rather, an increasing degree of personal detachment, along with a further merging of our aims and our concerns, and an increased level of communication will produce a growing universal consciousness.

When we fully grasp and incorporate what Copernicus and Galileo and the rest of 'em were saying, we will understand that we are not the be-all and end-all but just a part of the whole. And we will operate from the awareness that it is not the larger body that revolves around the smaller body, but the smaller body that revolves around the larger. Then it will be up to us to discern just what the larger body is, around which our movements are centered, and to realize that our connection to other smaller bodies is established through our connection to the larger body. And we will begin to see things not as they relate to us, and our problems, and our concerns, but, instead, as they relate to the whole. And our decisions will be less self-serving and more group-serving. And that will give a glimpse of a bigger picture, a larger truth.

February 11, 2001

Unleashing the arrow of aspiration

So much and nothing going through my mind at the same time.

I find myself thinking of things that are made more effective by virtue of the time and the conditions.

Take gardening, for instance; the act of preparing the ground, placing the seed into the soil and watering the plant as it grows. There are, without question, better and worse, more and less advantageous times for it. If we are looking to grow vegetables, it works better, seasonal exceptions notwithstanding, if we plant in early spring rather then late fall.

Taking vitamins is another example. It may or may not prove to be beneficial to our well-being to supplement our diet with vitamins. If, however, we're looking and hoping to improve our health through supplementation, then we would do well to take the vitamin pills when there is food in our system rather than on an empty stomach.

In baseball, a base hit when our team is up to bat is a good thing whenever it may occur. But it is especially good when we have runners in scoring position. For then, a hit produces a run, and it's the team with the most runs, not the most hits, that ultimately wins the game.

Or suppose we've hurt someone through something we've said or done, or wronged a person in some way. Apologizing can and often does start to make things better, but generally, only if the person we're apologizing to is there to hear us say I'm sorry.

And while the recipe for the bread may call for us to combine ingredients such as flour and yeast, it does no good to add the yeast after the flour has already been baked in the oven.

Timing is important. Some people even go so far as to say timing is everything. I don't say it, because I have witnessed how this idea, this held belief, can produce despair in people who feel they've somehow "missed the boat," or "blew their chance." I'm confident that there are several boats, and that we are afforded plenty of chances.

Nonetheless, I recognize the importance of timing. So when my friend, and also the voice of my own intuition, told me that now, right now, is an especially advantageous time for spiritual growth and development, I listened.

On what do I base this claim? Well, I could talk about the alignment of the stars, about prophecy, about the Great Wheel of Time, about the age of mankind, about south nodes and north nodes, and about the full eclipse in the sign of Capricorn, but would any of that convey the meaning, or shed light on why the time and the conditions are particularly beneficial? And is it even necessary? Do we require a full explanation and complete understanding of the internal combustion engine before we get in the car and drive? Is the study of electricity and magnetism a prerequisite for flicking on the light switch? And what about air travel? Can you explain exactly why that airplane stays up in the air? Some of us can and some of us can't. But that doesn't stop those of us who can't from getting on board. So, rather than attempting to put forth some complex esoteric explanation, I will, instead, merely note that it is springtime in the garden of the soul; that there are runners on second and third with one out; that the person who needs to hear what you have to say is listening; and that the oven has been properly preheated and all of the ingredients have been mixed together in proper proportion.

"Opportunity's precious," I wrote oh so many years ago.

"And time is a knife,
Conditions are right,
For a change in my life."
And I'm feeling it again. But, this time, it feels like the conditions are right not just for a change in my life but in all of ours.

Let not this opportunity pass on by without unleashing the arrow of aspiration from the bow of your heart, guided by the scope of your mind.

February 2001

Follow your heart
along the path of your soul

"Lose your mind 'cuz your heart's been found,
Shake 'em,
Shake 'em on down."

- Michael On Fire
"Shake 'Em on Down"

I have this friend who was a lawyer. But he didn't like being a lawyer. Correction: He liked being a lawyer, he just didn't like practicing law. So one day, shortly after he made junior partner in the highly regarded law firm where he worked, he decided that, instead, he wanted to be the harmonica player in his brother's band. Thing is, he didn't know how to play harmonica and his brother didn't have a band.

Some people thought he was losing his mind. I think he was finding his heart, and following it. And he's a happier man today for having done so.

Not that he ever did learn how to play the harmonica. But one thing led to the next, and followed from the other, and somehow, it all worked out.

They say that's what happens when you follow your heart. But what does that mean exactly? Does it mean doing whatever you want whenever you feel like it? Experience shows, and we teach our kids, that sometimes we have to deny ourselves in the short-run to get or to do something else we want even more in the long run. It's a matter of learning how to prolong the rewards.

Other people would suggest that "following your heart" is a matter of finding something you're really passionate about, and doing that thing. But again, this ignores the idea of multiple wants and desires.

For instance, in my case, a part of me, which I'll call "Ron the athlete," decides, after coming in from his workout at about three o'clock in the afternoon and regarding himself in the mirror before stepping into the shower, that it's time to tone the muscles and shed a few pounds. In order to accomplish this, he resolves to eat a little less and drink a little less and to do hundreds of push-ups and sit-ups each day. Then, at about midnight or so, another part of me, whom I'll call "Ron the writer," says, 'I know Ron the athlete made a commitment to shaping up, and I can dig it, but right now, I'm more concerned with getting this idea out and written down, and in order to do so I have to find a way to stay awake. So even though the plan was to skip the snacking in between meals, I'm just going to nibble on a few more of these, and have a couple more swigs of this and a taste of that,' and in that way, what was important to me in the afternoon becomes decidedly less important in the wee wee hours.

So you see, simply doing what you want to do or going where you want to go is not quite so simple as all that, or as some might make it out to be. At least not as long as you have all these different selves, or different parts of your self heading off in different directions. The work, then, becomes a matter of unification, or integration, and not just of body, mind and spirit, which is the usual wholistic admonishment, but of this multiplicity of selves as well.

It brings to mind this woman I know, who wakes up each morning, poised and ready to receive and respond to whatever words or message Spirit conveys to her. The only problem is Spirit seems to tell her something different, or so her mind would have her believe, almost every day. I call her the human pinball because she's constantly ricocheting around, bouncing from one thing to the next.

And that reminds me of something that happened to me years ago. I was in a nightclub, listening and dancing to the music. When the song was over, this old black man, who knew me and knew that I had ailing ankles, saw me hobbling back to my seat. He said, "You shouldn't be out there doing that."

"I know," I replied, "but my spirit is moving me to dance."

"Your spirit," he said, "is messing you up," only he didn't use the word "messing."

It was one of the funniest things I ever heard.

But what's not so funny is seeing people close off to the impulses of their heart, under the guise of being smart, as if disavowing the direct knowing we call intuition, which is the heart's way of perceiving, is in any way an intelligent thing to do.

There are those who like to ask and consider what it is that separates us from the animals. I am compelled to ask and consider what separates us from the machines we use to make our lives more convenient. And surely, the answer, at least in large part, has to do with the heart, and it's capacity to feel and to care.

There are some things the heart can discern that the mind cannot. Likewise, there are things that arouse the body that fulfill not the heart nor stimulate the mind. Clearly, to focus on or to follow only one of these levels of awareness, such as the heart, is to relegate oneself to partiality and incompleteness. We arrive at the totality of ourselves through an opening and merging of all our instruments of perception and levels of awareness.

And while I wholeheartedly rejoice in the opening and expanding of the heart, it is the path of the soul that leads to our greatest fulfillment and highest development.

So go on, follow your heart, and let it connect you to your passion and purpose. Let it open the door, and your mind, to reveal the path that leads you to you ... da you da you da you, and hi de hi de ho.

March 15, 2001

Poetry and feeling; bringing Life to life

Stepped outside to throw some clothes in the wash. It was late, and dark, and as I opened the door to our laundry room, I felt my heel crunch down on a snail and drag it a few inches across the concrete patio. It wasn't the first time it's ever happened, but to just let it go by, without even taking note of it, or acknowledging it in some way, seemed way too irreverent and insensitive so I went inside and jotted down a few-line poem. As that was a few days ago, and as I wrote the poem on some scrap piece of paper which is now nowhere to be found, I don't remember the exact wording, but I do recall the feeling, and that, I think, is the important thing. Otherwise, it, meaning Life, seems always somewhere off at a distance. And this little incident probably would have remained so too had it not found its way into a poem.

And the next night, I got poked in the eye, and I've been grappling to gain vision ever since. And as it was probably only the third time in my life that I haven't had sight, and only the second time I can remember, I thought it worth noting. Worth noting, also, are the other two times I haven't had sight.

The first time is the one I don't remember. It happened when I was three years old. I say that because my family says it happened when I was three or four, and I remember four but I don't remember three. What happened, I'm told, is that I was standing up in a wagon eating a popsicle, and my sister was pulling me around, and we hit a crack in the sidewalk, and I fell and, yep, you guessed it, the popsicle stick went into my eye, and it stuck there. They rushed me to the hospital, and there it got yanked out. And, I imagine, I must have had my sight interrupted at that point. And maybe, too, it was so mind-blowing that that's why I don't remember it and before.

The only other time my vision failed me was last fall when my eyes shut down after looking into a computer monitor for far too many nights and days in a row.

Other than these few times, though, my vision has been exceptional. In fact, along with my hands and my memory, my eyes are one of my two or three most outstanding traits.

But back to my being poked in the eye, I wrote down what I was going through in a few hasty lines and included it in the letter I sent off to my friend the poet, the pearl, whom I thank for keeping poetry in my life. The poem informed him that:
"The strangest stuff's been floating by,
Ever since I hurt my eye,
Looks like hairy black spaghetti,
Mixed with grey and white confetti,
It makes me dizzy, gets me sick,
Feels like someone's playn a trick,
And so I keep this black patch on,
Until this crazy stuff is gone."
And ever the poet, he wrote right back and said:
"Even if it's just a scratch,
Don't take off the patch."
And while crushed snails and pokes in the eye might not be the kind of lofty stuff some of us think of when we think of poetry, it's like the 19th Century writer and preacher, Frederick William Robertson, wrote:
"The office of poetry is not to make us think accurately, but feel truly."
There's that feeling thing again.
I think, maybe, the reason it's coming up to be emphasized

today, is because, for one, we're so embroiled in technology, which is wonderful but not a-Live, and so even though it connects us with worlds of information it does not necessarily further our connection to Life, and two, because in our effort to become more intelligent there has definitely been a polarization towards the head center, which is where thinking, not feeling, occurs, and so, much of the day, and much of our life, passes by unfelt.

And I mention poetry because jotting down even those few easy lines made the circumstances of my own life come alive for me.

There are people, I know, who feel, what with all that's going on, and all the information that's needing to be absorbed, that there just isn't time for poetry. But considering how it can bring Life to life, and stimulate the heart and soul in these times of body and mind, I, for one, resolve to make time.

Write On.
Read On.
Rave On.

March 26, 2001

Emptying the cup, and other common expressions

"Never put off till tomorrow what you can do today."

- Ben Franklin

I know, in my case, when there's something I'm really not looking forward to dealing with, a call that has to be made, an issue that needs to be addressed, something that needs to get straightened out, I have a tendency to put it off. And if I do, then what happens is that the nervous, gurgling feeling in my stomach that's keeping me from wanting to deal with it in the first place ends up staying with me even longer. And the thing is, it's not as if waiting a few extra hours, or a day, or whatever, is going to give me any extra insight or information into what to do and how to handle it. Maybe in some cases it will, but in most cases, I already know full well, or at least, plenty well enough, what I think and what I feel and what I want.

And when I just go ahead and deal with it, almost invariably, I end up feeling so much better. And not just better because the nervousness is gone, but better on account of no longer being debilitated by apprehension. Better for having cleared the table, and I end up reminding myself, time and time again, of the wisdom in emptying the cup that it may be filled.

It's a popular saying from a popular story, about a university professor who went to go visit the Zen master. His reason for going was, supposedly, to learn something from the master, but during his visit, he ends up doing more talking than listening, more showing off what he knows than finding out what the other guy is about, and focusing more on how far he's come rather than how far he has to go. As this is going on, the master offers his guest a cup of tea. The man accepts, so the master places a cup in front of him and begins to pour. And pour and pour, until the cup overflows and spills over on to the man's lap. The professor jumps back and says – "What're you doing? Can't you see the cup is full and can't hold any more?" The master says something to the effect of, "Likewise, your cup is full and can't hold any more. Until you empty your cup, I am unable to teach you anything."

It has to do with the idea of newness. New ideas, new insights, new circumstances, new challenges, new encounters, a new way, a new world, new horizons and a new day-dawning. And who among us isn't up, or down, depending on your dialect, for that kind of thing? But, though many of us may want to become new, we're not always so keen on letting go of the old. And some of us ask, why should I let go of it? Am I just supposed to disregard everything I've learned, and earned, and fought to acquire up to this point? And the answer is, of course not, for the recommendation to empty your cup has not so much to do with knowledge, wisdom and experience as it does with attitude.

Which is not at all to suggest that there's a right and wrong way of acting and reacting, and that one is an indication of a good attitude and the other is a sign of a bad attitude. The kind of attitude I'm talking about is one of openness, willingness and humility. It's being open to a truth that may, and likely does, extend beyond the boundary of beliefs, opinions and past experiences. It's being willing to keep learning and growing, and gaining a deeper insight and appreciation. It's a humility that allows you to admit that as long as you're still here walking around on this earth, breathing the air, taking up space, contained, still, within the confines of skin and bones, that you're not all-knowing, all-wise and all-powerful. And so, you *humbly* and *willingly* open yourself to greater knowledge, deeper wisdom and higher power.

It's understanding that the great teacher in life is Life, and realizing that our learning depends, in large part, on our being present for the lesson. Being present in the present. It's knowing and noting that things rarely turn out as we plan. And with that as a reminder, it's being willing to move forward into an uncertain future. And even if the movements are not quite so energetic, but more akin to just waiting patiently and biding the time, it's a matter of somehow quelling the fears and remaining *open* to the unfolding events that constitute the path of the soul, which is a unique journey.

And, I suppose, that's what this whole thing really comes down to – reveling in the journey ...

Which sounds easy but ain't, as long as fear persists.

March 28, 2001

Craving the connection to my creative compadres

Brother to brother,
Searching for something,
Partners in crime,
Friend to friend,"
      - Michael On Fire
      "Your Ears Must Be Burning"

It's not a matter of wanting to go back in time, this deep desire I have to call a hundred friends, for the moments, the fellowship and the communion I'm wishing to connect with exist out of time. They represent critical events that served to springboard me in the direction of my dreams, which is a realm of wonder and creativity.

Unattached to any particular achievements, outcomes or morals-of-the-story, they are the descriptions in an unwritten journal; the colors and contours, the shapes and textures revealed in the paintings that hang in my own private, personal museum. Portraits of myself and others from various initiation ceremonies. Like graduation pictures, or vacation photos, only these exist not on some flat two-dimensional surface, rather, they float in forever space and forever feeling.

Enduring episodes that were formed and that first came to light not in and of the big, spectacular events, not from the scheduled occasions or the planned happenings, and not from the destinations, but from the impromptu interactions of the unsuspecting in-betweens, which are but moments along the journey. Images marked by unspoken vows and undeclared pledges — to ever-expanding consciousness, and to the ceaseless broadening of horizons. Moments of mutual appreciation; parallel movements; hints of something different that, we decided, was something we shared in common.

It's the lengthy philosophical discussions, the evolution of shared language, the familiar references, the inside jokes, the abstract excursions, and all the music we've loved and shared. It's the journeys we've taken, the sights we've seen and the impressions we were left with. It's the things we discovered, both without and within, about ourselves and each other. It's the obstacles we've overcome.

It's the way we've joined forces in righteous rebellion, and it's the ideals we aspire to.

It's all-night walks and all-night talks, and pour-your-heart-out letters and phone conversations.

It's the close-calls, and the far-reaching plans. It's little victories, big dreams and even bigger disappointments.

It's things we tried for the very first time together.

It's things we know about each other, but overlook anyway.

It's the mysteries and the marvels and the miracles we've beheld.

It's the manner in which we've kept each other encouraged and inspired, and the way in which we just don't buy it from each other.

It's the times and the ways we've been able to make each other feel a little less alone.

It's people I've known my whole life, or if not then darn near, and others whom I've shared maybe a day and a couple of letters with.

It's a person who is floating to me, now, in some unknown nether region that exists somewhere between state capitals, and, evidently, too, between guilt and renunciation. It's someone else whose whereabouts I do know but who remains out of reach nonetheless. It's the one I've never heard from, or about, again, and many others with whom the exchange is ongoing. And it's a pair of pals I can't call, cuz' they can't talk on the phone.

These are the objects of my yearning, the people and places and treasures I'm turning towards through time. And even though I'm craving the connection, and wanting to re-animate the meaning of those magic moments, at the same time, I'm not much in the mood for talking about myself and "what's going on these days," nor for listening too long about what's going on on their end. And so I write, rather than call, unfinished letters that won't get sent, and cherish the memories and the exchanges that I'm guessing will stay with me forever.

"There are places I'll remember,
All my life, though some have changed,
Some forever, not for better,
Some are gone, and some remain,
All these places have their moments,
With lovers and friends, I still can recall,
Some are dead and some are living,
In My Life, I've loved them all"

\- John Lennon
"In My Life"

April 3, 2001

The Internet; a tool or a crutch?

In sports, when a team loses a game they were favored to win, the coaches frame the experience as "a wake-up call." Other times, *a medical emergency* can be a wake-up call, alerting a person that he or she may need to change their way of eating, thinking, or not recreating if they want to remain around for a while. Still other times, a near miss, like for instance, an almost auto accident that was just barely averted, can be a wake-up call that you better pay more attention to the road. I had my own kind of wake-up call this week. It had to do with how I get my information.

Lately, I've been in the habit of getting on the Internet and surfing the world wide web to see what I come across, what interesting tidbits might spur my thoughts and imagination, as a way of coming up with topics to write about. It's often not even a direct connection, it's just that one thing leads to another and before you know it I'm off and running.

This past week, however, I have been unable to get online and access the sites I normally visit. At first, that is, during the first few days of having this process interrupted, I let it detain me, even though I realized how ridiculous that is.

The Internet has been called a tool, and indeed, it is an incredible tool, but it is also a crutch, and like the crutches we use when we injure a leg or a foot, if it is used beyond the point of needed support, or if it is relied upon too much then it serves to weaken us. In the case of the leg injury, if we lean on the crutch for too long a time, we run the risk of having our muscles atrophy. In the case of the Internet, it's our thinking and our feeling and our imagination that are in jeopardy of withering.

It is not so unlike what happened in the area of health and

healing. As medicine grew ever more sophisticated and ever more amazing, people started to completely turn over their health and well-being to doctors. A lot of people got to thinking — whatever it is, I'll just take some pill for it and it'll make it better. They disregarded the power *they have* in terms of diet and exercise and proper rest and prayer and meditation, and things like that. Instead, they gave their power away to doctors and hospitals and insurance companies. It's turning back around now, where people are taking much more of an active role in their own health and healing.

Health care is but one of the myriad examples of people "relinquishing power."

One of the things we see and hear a lot of these days is how education advocates are pushing hard to see that every classroom in our schools is Internet-connected. Sure, we all need the skills, resources and opportunities to succeed, but having all of our classrooms wired together is, I believe, far less important than the matter of teaching children how to think ... independently ... for themselves. I don't mean how to come up with the answer to a question on a test, or even where to go to find the answer to that question, but rather, how to come up with a thought of their own, how to recognize and identify their own feelings, and how to imagine something. How to activate their senses so as to more fully perceive the life rhythm of the world. These things are not stressed, nor are they mandated, because they are abstract and ethereal.

We'll gladly find a way to raise and spend gazillions of dollars on computer equipment, but I doubt we would ever consider paying teachers even a fraction of that amount for doing the all-important job of turning out independent thinkers. It reminds me of the line from the bible about the people who "put their faith in horses and chariots," again, referring to the equipment and machinery. It's yet another example of society placing more emphasis on the outer than on the inner.

The question is often asked – How will technology change our lives in the future? As far as this technology goes, the answer may depend on whether we use it as a tool or as a crutch, for that may determine whether we grow stronger and continue to develop, mentally speaking, or whether we weaken and decline.

The Internet is like the vitamins we buy off the store shelves. That is, it has value as a supplement, not a substitute.

Now, if I can only keep that in mind.

April 5, 2001

Tales of the town square,
the health of the heart

Wandering aimlessly
With no place to be
Just looking for stories to tell

Even though I had more than 60 miles to go, I detoured off the highway at a place I never had before just to see where it would take me. I knew I would be heading generally in the right direction, and I knew I would be able to get back to where I needed to be in the event that I happened to get lost. But that's the point; I did need to get lost. I needed to lose myself, and find something else in the process, and I was hoping that some new sights and new scenery might just be the thing to stir up some new impressions.

A few hours later, the Universe delivered up just what the soul-doctor ordered, and it came in the form of a town square. That is, a city park a square-block or two big, around and through which, were sidewalks and walkways. And they were being used too, and at a most leisurely pace, by people of all ages, though not a lot of people, as it was a rainy afternoon. And there was grass, and big old trees, and a cement ledge around an area of plants and flowers and bushes, which served as a place for people to sit; for people to talk and visit, to rest, to watch, to take it all in and be a part of it.

It reminded me of the central-park in the town next to the town I grew up in. Once I got my license I started going there often because it was alive and wondrous and a lot cooler than my town. What made it so was that it was defined by so much more than just its city limits and its geographical borders. There was something special about the way it retained its culture and supported its humanity.

I remember being there one night, late, and encountering this mysterious man leaning up against the lamppost on the corner, reading poetry 'neath the street light. And he gave me an appreciation of it, though it is the visual image of him standing there reading, more so than the words, that has stayed with me all these years.

Next to strike me about this new, for me, park I landed in, was the delightful old-fashioned gazebo-type band shell, like the kind that was in the park in "Pepper-land;" the same kind we've performed on in numerous towns around the country. Recalling those events, I knew that here was a town that provided its people with music, and with opportunities to be together just for the enjoyment of it and just for the sake of being together. It conjured up episodes along the Mississippi River, and Memorial Days spent in Galena, Ill.

And then there was the public library, with the concrete steps leading up to it, which reminded me of the time we broke down, and got stranded in LaGrange, Kentucky, and how I went to work there on some stranger's farm, and how each day and each new disappointment got more bizarre and more unbelievable.

And there was the movie theater, and the restaurants and the pubs, and the shops with the canvas awnings and the big picture windows lining the way. When it started raining harder, I ducked inside to ponder it over a pint, and as I listened to the music on the juke box, and gazed out the rain-streaked windows, it felt a whole lot like that place in Ames, Iowa, or was it Cedar Falls?

And after I spent the few bucks I had, and continued on my way, the sidewalks carried me through Placerville, and Riverside, Santa Rosa, Otsego, Manchester and a hundred other towns I've never been to.

If it was stories I was seeking, there were plenty coming at me now. Tales of the town square, and how it connects people together who, maybe, have nothing more in common than just the simple fact of being there. In this case, whether or not any of us who were there supported the same causes, or voted for the same candidates, or belonged to the same organizations made no difference whatsoever. Neither did it matter if we liked the same things or not, because each of us, through our presence there, is what made the picture complete.

The town square represents the heart of the village.

It's no wonder heart disease is the leading killer in this country, because for so long, we turned our collective backs on the heart. Instead, we put up a bunch of strip malls, and fast-food restaurants, and cold, characterless structures that cut us off from our cultural heritage and from each other.

This is not intended as a commentary on city planning, or as a primer on environmental psychology, however, it seems clear that when we lose the center, and take away opportunities and venues for relaxed, meaningful human interaction, the disintegration of the community is sure to follow.

Today, "heart-health" is a prevalent and popular topic and concern. More and more people are making the effort to control their intake of saturated fats, and high-sodium, high-cholesterol foods, while at the same time, increasing their intake of foods rich in antioxidants. People are smoking less and exercising more, and paying attention to things that increase the amount of stress in their lives. Even our restaurants have little symbols on the menus to indicate which things are good for the heart. As we continue to work to reduce the instances of coronary disease, let us not forget, also, to pay attention to the heart of the village, the strengthening of the community, the preservation of our culture(s), and the perpetuation of our tales.

April 10, 2001

Dealing with temptation down in the shop

"The temptation is not here, where you are reading about it or praying about it. It is down in your shop, among bales and boxes, ten-penny nails, and sandpaper."

- Edwin Hubbel Chapin

I know exactly what he means, because it ended up getting me "down in the shop," as Chapin would say.

It all went down before I even knew what was happening, and it wasn't until afterwards that I realized what I was dealing with. Temptation with a capital T, but it was different ...

... Not at all like the kind Stevie Wonder sang about in his song "I Wish," where he goes:

"You grow up and learn that kinda thing ain't right,
But while you were doing it, it sure felt outta sight."

It wasn't at all like that, for this didn't bring any pleasure or excitement, not even in the moment.

I didn't know, when I was telling her what I knew, that I was gossiping. I was just trying to bond and be friends, but before you know it, the thing was spreading like wildfire. I wished I could have taken it back but I know that words spoken in haste, like the arrow once loosed from the bow, and kisses too, cannot be taken back.

It wasn't that I was saying anything that was untrue, nor was I attacking anybody, but I came to see, though not until afterwards, that the telling of the words served no constructive purpose whatsoever, and, on the contrary, only served to create a rift. Even though the rift wasn't obvious or easily detectable, I could feel it nonetheless, and it didn't feel good to have been segregation's henchman. Because, to me, the great task at this time, both on a personal and a planetary level, has to do with integration, unification, bringing people together and forming the parts into a whole. It didn't take a super sleuth to discover that my joining in on the yappity-yap wasn't serving the grand task, and for that I felt remorse.

Later in the day, as I walked around town, it was still with me and hard to shake. I searched for similes to describe the allure of that desire to bond, and also how it felt once I knew that I had already said too much. "It's like quicksand," I decided at first, "the way it pulls you in and pulls you down," not that I've ever been in quicksand, though I have been in some powerful mud bogs. Nobody intentionally steps into quicksand, I told myself, it just catches you unsuspecting-like, and then (if the movies are to be believed) you have to struggle to try and extricate yourself. Then I thought how it was also like the apple in the garden; the thing we're not supposed to do, but we go ahead and do anyway. It's like Moses Adams said, in his Civil War diary: "I see the devil's hook, and yet cannot help nibbling at his bait."

Suddenly, I was hearing my heart cry out, "Lord, lead us not into temptation." And there I was dealing with it, not in some big, theoretical way, not in terms of some definite and unchanging list of do's and don't's, but rather, in terms of my own conscience. What made it wrong was that it didn't feel right, and that was the only indicator I needed to tell me I did not want to repeat it again any time soon.

Today it was gossip, tomorrow it will, undoubtedly, be something else, because for each virtue we aspire to, we encounter a corresponding temptation. I'm not so much concerned with all the ones "out there," it's the ones "in here" that concern me. The key, I believe, is going to be keeping the purpose in mind and burning strong in the center, more of the time. That way, actions and decisions can be seen and felt in relation to the purpose, and temptation can be sorted out in terms of whether the thing being considered supports or undermines the object of my aspiration.

April 19, 2001

Learning to live and learning to die

"I was screaming at the top of my lungs, and I swear it felt like I was gonna die," she said, while describing the experience she had last week on the big roller coaster at the big amusement park.

And then she said, "What is it that makes us pay money and stand in line for an hour-and-a-half so we can experience something that makes us feel like we're gonna die?"

Seeing as I'm not the kind of guy who has ever gone in much for those types of rides, I'm not sure I'm qualified to render an opinion on what it was she was asking. Nevertheless, it got me thinking about how learning to die, and by that I mean preparing ourselves for the transition process we have come to call death, might be one of, if not, THEE most important thing we can learn in this life. And it brought to mind a guy I met many years ago who was going around teaching people how to die.

He had some experience in this, see, dating back to 1961, when both his lungs collapsed simultaneously, and an ambulance was called on to the scene. When they arrived, they found him unconscious, with no pulse, and his breathing had stopped. They tried reviving him, but to no avail, so he was "officially pronounced dead." But according to him, he was perfectly aware of what was going on, he was just too comfortable to do anything about it. Until they were carrying him down the stairs on a stretcher, which is when he threw back the sheet that had been pulled up over his face. They rushed him to the hospital and then later that night and again the next day they went through the whole thing again (and again), where they pronounced him dead and he came back.

Once his lungs resumed normal functioning they sent him home. After a few more weeks and a few more times of dying and coming back, without any trained medical personnel around, his wife decided she'd had enough. She thought he was some kind of ghoul or something so she left him.

But while it may have frightened others around him, it had the exact opposite affect on him. That is, it made him less afraid. For one thing, he no longer feared death, and why should he? He had already been dead and he found it to be perfectly peaceful. Not only that, but the fact that he remained conscious even after he died was, for him, highly empowering. It convinced him that though we withdraw from our bodies at some point in time, still we continue to exist, only in a different way and on a different plane.

In the 18 years that followed his "near-death" experiences,

the man proceeded, in his words, to die thousands of times, at first accidentally, and then later, consciously.

It reminded me then, and still does, of the various books "of the dead," including the Tibetan, the Egyptian, the Hebrew and the Mayan, all of which are sort of like instruction manuals for dying. In each of these texts, death is described as a matter of consciousness, and the "art of dying" is the conscious ability to make a smooth transition from one plane to another.

What makes the whole thing so terrifying for so many people, said this man who, according to medical science, had already experienced death, is that they/we are so attached to the physical plane and to material consciousness. We're afraid of being alone, he said, and of losing that which is familiar to us.

So what he did, is he started teaching others a technique for letting go of the things of this world. By giving verbal directions he would help people enter a hyper-relaxed state. Then, he would get them to visualize and consider in great detail, first their most prized possessions, then the people they love the most, and finally, their own body and body-parts and bodily-functions and sensations. And in each case, he would then have them see the object disappear right out of existence.

I was laying there going through this, and there was a woman lying next to me, and several others in the room too, who were, literally, screaming and crying, so terrified were they by this "letting go" exercise.

And, I imagine, it's kind of how my friend sounded when she was hurtling 85 miles an hour down the steep incline from the very front seat of the dare-devilish ride. And it prompted me to consider whether there was a correlation between these two methods of simulating dying. Perhaps the purpose of both, I thought, is to make us less afraid, of dying and of living.

Then again, maybe the real value doesn't have a whole lot to do with death but, rather, with giving us a fuller appreciation of life.

"If we wish to die well we must learn to live well."
– Dalai Lama

April 23, 2001

In search of greener pastures

We were driving around and we saw a horse, a field of grass and a barbed-wire fence. The grass was near knee-high for about as far as we could see on both sides of the fence. The horse had her head sticking through the top two strands of the three-stranded fence, to the point where the barbs were jabbing hard into her neck, and she gobbled the grass outside the fence, which looked exactly like the grass inside the fence. And my gal said, "Talk about a perfect example of the grass always being greener on the other side." And she was right, for indeed it was a case of a picture speaking a thousand words. I wished I'd had a camera. I would have photographed it and hung the picture up as a constant reminder to myself. Instead, I'll just have to remember it on my own.

It's an old story with a familiar moral, but one that many of us still grapple with. Most often, it's considered in the context of "wanting what the other guy has," and in that sense, it often gets connected with the 10th Commandment. The one about coveting what your neighbor has, whether it's his house, his wife, his ox or anything else. And while some of us sometimes do get to thinking how lucky that other fellow is, and are prone on occasion to wish for what he has, maybe not his possessions but his options and opportunities, it need not necessarily have to do with others. It can be entirely, or more or less, about ourselves. Meaning, we find something that ignites our passion or our sense of purpose or makes us feel more alive and more fulfilled, and, not surprisingly we want more of it. And we want less of whatever takes us away from it. Or maybe that's just us dreamers, I don't know. To me, it seems natural and noble to seek a path that leads to greater expression, deeper joy and fuller appreciation. It's what we call following your heart, or at least being able to hear its call. And I hope that each and every one of us can find the vision, the strength, the wherewithal, or whatever it takes and whatever it involves to make a change should we find ourselves in a situation that is not nourishing our heart, not feeding our soul, and not allowing us to be ourselves. Whether that means inner change or outer change.

Where the "grass is greener" part comes in is when we start desiring a "different life," someone else's perhaps, because we believe it will eliminate all conflict, resistance and distractions. But we forget that *conflict when resolved leads to wisdom, and resistance when overcome builds character*. As long as there are other people in the world there are going to be distractions. So we'd best learn how to focus through them rather than attempting to eliminate them altogether.

Which is not at all to suggest that we should just "grin and bear it" no matter what the case may be. It is only to put forth a reminder that we are each unique beings, all parts of an incredible whole, and that the particular lessons that are each of ours to learn in this lifetime can only be learned through the experiences that come to us along our particular paths.

The pasture that is greener, for sure, is the one where we can most wholly be ourselves and be our most holy selves.

Wholeness and Holiness - both entail a state of connectedness.

Wholeness, on a personal level, implies unity of being, oneness of body, mind and spirit, integration of our various aspects, aims and talents. On an interpersonal level, the connection involves the formation of interdependent relationships and meaningful associations within a group or a community.

Holiness, too, involves connection — to higher purpose; oneness with the Universe; accordance with divine will.

And as there are whole and holy people in all walks of life, and from every social and economic situation, clearly, it has nothing to do with where you are and what you do. It's an awareness, a state of being. Though, clearly too, being somewhere you love doing something you love makes it a whole lot easier to feel whole and holy.

So, yes, let's continue to aspire towards improvement and advancement and strive to make things better, but in the course of doing so let's not get bogged down focusing on the bad things to the point that we neglect to recognize and appreciate all the good things. For it is a great blessing to be aware of small blessings.

April 30, 2001

Making a point out of being alive

Hearing myself and others moan the way we sometimes do, it almost seems that we spend as much energy, thought and time trying to get away from our lives as we do trying to get to or at them.

And it's not that we're trying to get away from our lives, just that part of our living that doesn't make us feel so alive.

Which, brings to mind something that motivation champ Tony Robbins said. He advised people not to spend more than 15 percent of the time on the problem, which leaves 85 percent of the time for the solution. And with that simple guideline in mind, I made the decision to not spend the thinking time that precedes the writing time pondering what *doesn't* make us feel alive. Instead, I turned my attention towards that which *does* make us feel alive.

One of the things that certainly does it for me is when I feel like I'm sharing my gifts. And looking around, I think I can detect the same kind of thing in others. In the chef, for instance, who pours her ideas and her love out into her culinary creations and then gets to see people enjoying them. In the healer who pours his care and his training out through his touch, and then gets to see the results and feel the gratitude. In the singers who pour their soul and talent out into a song and get, in return, quiet listening and loud applause. In the coaches who pour their knowledge and experience into players, and then get to witness the development of skill and character. In all walks of and in all fields of endeavor, we all like to feel that we're giving and receiving something.

'Lest we forget, though, the first and foremost of our gifts, more basic even than any of our prime passions, is the gift of life. To share this gift requires neither opportunity nor permission, only that we commit to being alive.

What does commitment have to do with it, you may wonder. And you might say, "There are plenty of people," and you might even add, "myself included," who are here and walking around without having made a commitment to being alive. But it is worth asking if the mere fact of existence, of taking up space and air, is being alive any more than people being in the same place at the same time and doing the same thing constitutes sharing.

I think here of driving in rush hour traffic, which for many is a daily ritual. A lot of people are doing it at the same time but that doesn't mean they're sharing. Maybe if people are in the same vehicle then we can speak of them sharing that experience, but otherwise, most of the people are not even aware of each other beyond the demands of road safety.

The word sharing connotes joint participation and also mutual appreciation. To get a better understanding of these words, and a clearer picture of what it means to share, consider the idea of opposites. As darkness reveals light, and sound needs quiet in order to be heard, likewise, I get a stronger feeling for what it means to participate and appreciate by considering what it means to "not participate" and "not appreciate."

Consider words like "withhold," "reject," "deny," "decline," "stay away from," "refuse to give" and "say no to." None of these, by themselves, are adequate antonyms to the word "participate," but all of them, taken together, get across the meaning of "not participating." And while it is courageous to not participate in that which goes against one's conscience, it is life and not some destructive activity we're talking about participating in here. As for not appreciating, it implies not acknowledging, not recognizing the value of, and not being grateful for.

These days, we've got computers and other electronic devices, and organizers and calendars, and whatever other systems and methods we might use to remind us of all that has to be done. Sometimes we get so busy attending to all the rest of it that we forget about some of the most basic stuff, like simply making sure to live and learn from life each and every day. It seems silly to say, but go ahead, put it on your "Things To Do" list. Make it a priority to be alive; to participate in and appreciate the great gift of life.

May 2001

When deciding 'if the shoe fits'
isn't so simple

I'm in a terrible fix, the likes of which I've never known before.

My problem is I can't seem to find a pair of shoes, at least not a pair of new ones. I've got plenty of old ones, too many in fact, spilling out of my closet, with holes in the soles, and raggedy laces full of knots from all the times they've torn, and heels that are worn, and sides that are scuffed.

It's weird. I can go for weeks and months on end and never feel the need to wash my truck, but not so with my shoes. Ever since I've been 12 years old, when I got that pair of two-toned boots from Scott Coburn's Saddlery and Western Shop, I've loved going through the ritual of shining my shoes. I've got a bag full of Kiwi tins and old socks and wash cloths and T-shirts that I use to put the polish on, and brushes of various sizes, and mink oil, and bear grease, and Propert's conditioners, and two different weather-proofers and a spot remover. It's not like I'm fanatical about it, or that anyone could ever mistake me for being a dress-up kind of guy, but I like my shoes to look good, at least in my eyes. And therein lies the root of my problem.

See, I can't stand the way most of the shoes look that are out these days. In my opinion, we are at an all-time low in shoe fashion. And it's even worse for men than for women.

I was out shopping this past weekend. After having already checked out all the shoe places in my small town, and a number of the ones in the larger cities to the north and south of me, I decided to go to the big mall in the big city. On my way there, as I was driving the main drag, I was checking out the shoes of the people walking on the sidewalk, and I didn't see anything I liked; nothing that made me go – yeah, those look pretty cool.

And then, when I got to the mall with the three large department stores, guess how many men's shoe stores I found – three, and they were all in the department stores, so they all carried the same style shoes. There was one other store that sold beach-type footwear and two that sold athletic shoes – but I wanted something slightly dressier than that; something that could be one of just two pair of shoes I might go on a trip with, the other being athletic shoes. No such luck.

The problem I'm running into, and this is after having bought four pair of new shoes in the last three months, is that either they're comfortable but I can't stand the way they look, which in turn makes me uncomfortable, or they look halfway decent to me but they hurt my feet, which is also uncomfortable.

Three months ago, I bought a pair of athletic shoes, and they're great but not quite dressy enough for what I want. Then, two months ago, while I was out of town for a few days, I bought another pair, but they're a little too dressy for day-in day-out. So, last month, I bought a pair that are dressier than the running shoes though not as comfortable, and more casual and more comfortable than the dressier pair but so gawky-looking to me that after wearing them around for a few hours I get so bugged that it becomes a drag.

After leaving the mall, and driving around through three other sections of town, I found a pair that looked good to me. They had them in stock in size seven and size 13-1/2. I'm no-where close to either of those, but I found out they had another store a few miles away. So I went and checked it out. Turns out they had seven pair in my size. Three were in a color I didn't want to buy. Three had a different "finish" than the pair that caught my eye, and the last pair looked perfect. But when I tried them on they were tight.

I spent an hour going back and forth – wrong color and comfortable, wrong finish and a little loose, and right-looking and tight-fitting. I tried every one of them on three times, four times, five times, and I finally settled on the good-looking pair.

I wore them out of the store and within five minutes I had blisters on my feet. Here I am, four days later, still trying to stretch them out.

Between the blisters and all these shoes I'm feeling like a combination Huck Finn/Imelda Marcos.

I figure, I gave the comfortable clodhoppers a few weeks, now I'm going to do the same with the fashionable foot-pinchers.

It's tempting, I know, to call it vanity, and to classify this as a classic case of image versus essence, form versus content, fashion versus comfort, but that would not be accurate for the comfortable ones aren't that comfortable and the good-looking ones aren't that good looking.

I'm reminded of the old adage – "If the shoe fits wear it." The thing is, my feet aren't the same size as my sense of style, and what fits the one doesn't necessarily fit the other. And I'm still feeling out which one is more uncomfortable being pinched.

May 17, 2001

The givers of life,
the nurturers of love

Mother: that which has given birth to or nurtures something.

Birth: beginning of anything; origin.

Origin: source from which something derives; root or cause.

Cause: that which makes something happen.

Happen: to come into being or occur.

Being: existence; life.

Life: the characteristics of life that are shared by all living organisms are growth, reproduction, metabolism, and the capacity to respond to stimuli.

Capacity: the faculty or potential for treating, experiencing, or appreciating.

Experiencing: the fact or state of having been affected by or gained knowledge through direct observation or participation.

Direct: Without obstruction or intervening influence.

Intervening: the condition of coming between.

Coming: arriving at a particular place, end, result, or conclusion.

Arriving: reaching a destination.

Destination: the purpose for which something is destined.

Purpose: the reason for which something is made or exists.

Made: past tense of make.

Make: to create.

Create: to bring into being.

Being: existence; life.

Life: a principle or force that is considered to underlie the distinctive quality of animate beings.

Force: strength, energy, dynamic quality.

Dynamic: relating to energy in motion.

Motion: process of changing position or place.

Process: series of continuous changes or actions that lead to a specific end.

Continuous: marked by uninterrupted extension in space, time, or sequence.

Extension: an enlargement in scope.

Scope: range within which something operates or applies.

Operate: to produce an intended or proper effect.

Produce: to cause to have existence or to happen.

Cause: a person or thing that is the occasion of an action or state.

Occasion: a special event or ceremony; a celebration:

Celebration: the observance of a holiday, performance of a religious ceremony, or participation in a festival.

Holiday: derived from "holy day;" a day marked by a general suspension of usual occupations in commemoration of a special event. In the United States, there are unofficially 15 national holidays, 10 of which are classified federal holidays. On federal holidays, federal and state offices, banks, schools, and businesses all over the country close down.

Some of the holidays, like Easter and Christmas, are religious holidays, and since not everyone is the same religion, not everyone celebrates them. Some, like Memorial Day, Veteran's Day and the Fourth of July, are patriotic holidays, and again, differences in ideologies means that not everyone celebrates. There are holidays commemorating famous people, and working people, and ones that mark a special day on the calendar. Celebration of each of them, except for one, is subject to a person's beliefs and observances. The only holiday that everybody in this country can truly all celebrate together is Mother's Day, for the fact that we were all born into this world is the one thing we all share in common.

Life may well be the gift of God, but it is given to us through the labor of a woman. And so we celebrate that on Mother's Day. And further, we celebrate the love and the care of the special women in our lives who bring life to life, whether or not there is a biological connection and whether the conception took place on the physical or some other plane. And might I suggest, too, that we go further still to honor and celebrate our mother, the earth, for her endless embrace and the inconceivable gifts that are continually bestowed upon us.

So whether it's mom, mama, ma, maw, mammy, memere, the mother country, the mother church or Mother Nature, remember the givers of life the nurturers of love.

May 28, 2001

A bit bugged by my reaction to the ants

Well, I definitely ain't no Albert Schweitzer.

If I recall correctly, he once told a young boy who was about to squash a fly in his bare hands, "Be careful with that fly. It's mine you know, and I'm afraid you might crush its wings."

Oh sure, I might feel like that at times, but seems like when it gets right down to the nitty gritty the barbarian in me comes out.

Yesterday, for instance, when I returned home from a four-day trip and found my house overrun by ants. I'm not talking about a few ants here and there inside the house, I'm talking overrun. The counters, the cupboards, the carpet too, were crawling with the little brown buggers, and my skin was crawling too. I figured, well, this must mean that our place is in need of a major cleaning, and so that's what I did. I unplugged the fridge and disconnected the stove and moved them both out of the way, and cleaned and cleaned. And I cleared off all the shelves in the kitchen, and rubbed and scrubbed and disinfected from floor to ceiling, and vacuumed in the living room too, but it didn't make a bit of difference. The things were still marching in droves practically everywhere I looked.

I remember hearing somewhere that if you mix dishwashing soap with water and spray it on the ants that it halts their further progress into the household. So I tried it once, twice, three and four times, but the reinforcements just kept arriving. I tried to make a pact with them, but I got the feeling it was strictly a unilateral treaty. Then I looked it up on the Internet, and found a bunch of sites about ants and what to do about them. One of the suggestions that showed up over and over again was to use mint. So I brewed up a pot of mint tea, put it in a spray bottle and sprayed it all around the counters and the cupboards. And when I woke in the morning, wouldn't you know it, the situation was twice as bad as when I went to bed, and my nerves were frayed and my patience was gone.

With dogs and a small daughter in the house, it never even occurred to me to spray poison in the place to keep the ants away but after not being able to sleep because it felt like ants were crawling all over me, and after having already cleaned and re-cleaned my kitchen four or five times only to see things get worse and worse, well, darned if I didn't drive straight to the hardware store and buy a can of the hard stuff; insecticide. The kind that says right on the label that it's hazardous to humans and domestic pets. The fact that it worked so quickly and so completely didn't make me feel any better.

I was reminded of "The Rest Of It," which was a screenplay I helped write when I was working for Stephen Stills. It was his story, which he came up with while hanging on a submarine during a USO tour. In it he asks, "How do we deal with them without becoming them?" He was talking about international terrorists, but after watching myself resort to such cold-hearted extermination tactics, I couldn't help but feel that in trying to deal with a situation, I had become somewhat sullied by it.

A bit later, I also remembered an encounter I had years ago with an old man in Northern Arizona. When I showed up with a bag of groceries, he was out in the field working with a hoe. His crops looked pretty ragged and eaten away, but far from being bummed out about it, he remained philosophical, saying, "The rats are my brothers, and they have to eat too." I was wishing I could remain as peaceful and as understanding as that, but I didn't. I snapped.

And I saw clearly, how people snap. How, when you see something over and over, or how when you're pushed once too often or a little too far, you can easily go to extremes. And it can cause you to think or act in ways that you might not otherwise. Like, for instance, you might start harboring and possibly even spewing off some bigoted generalizations. Or, as was the case with me, you might start spraying poison inside your home to wipe out a bunch of ants.

I can reconcile it easy enough, that's not the problem. The point that hit home so plain and simple through this ant episode has to do with aspiration, and how striving to be a conscious man or a conscious woman isn't just some part-time pursuit. It entails a great effort of seeking and finding creative solutions even when it's not necessarily convenient to do so. In other words, it's walking the walk.

June 1, 2001

Together in time; synchronization and synchronicity

It was one of those days where everything seemed to be so completely in synch you could almost trace the grand design.

For instance, twice, within the span of about 20 minutes I got the notion to call someone, or in this case two different someones, and both times, the person I intended on calling showed up a minute or so later right where I was. Mind you, these are not people I see all that often or with any regularity, and it wasn't the kind of thing where I know every Thursday at 1:30 so-and-so is likely to be in such-and-such a place. Then, two other times during the day, I thought about two other people who live far away, one a friend and one a business contact, and both times, the people I was thinking of called me on the telephone almost immediately afterwards. And still two other times, I thought I saw a particular someone in a crowd only to realize that the person I was seeing wasn't the person I thought it was. Then, when I turned and continued on, once on foot and once in the car, within a few seconds I ended up seeing the exact person I thought I was seeing in the other place.

It was all so uncanny, it made me wonder whether it was a case of me being more tuned in than usual or whether the universe was having a particularly magical day.

And while I love thinking about the world, indeed the universe, as a living breathing being which, like the living beings that comprise it, changes from day to day, I chose, rather, not to go there. Not to think about the universe itself having good and bad days, only because I knew that while I was walking through wonderland there were brothers and sisters in the Midwest who were going through a trying and somewhat frightening day due to the tornadoes that were whipping through their town. And others in the Mideast who were living in what Keith called "a crossfire hurricane" of hostility. And though it is a topic certainly worth ruminating upon, my thoughts moved instead to the dynamics of synchronicity; the concept of "meaningful coincidence," which has been discussed by everyone from Carl Jung to the Vedic philosophers to the Celestine prophets.

I've given a lot of thought to it myself and thought about it in a lot of different ways, but on this day, my conception began, simply, with the idea of "synchronizing your watches."

You always see it in those slick "heist" movies, how, in order to ensure precision and make certain that they're operating together in time, the gang of thieves will synchronize their watches. Or, as another example, musicians who, before the performance, tune up their instruments so that they will, at least, be in accordance from a physical "sound" standpoint. Whether or not they're able to get there on mental, emotional and spiritual levels as well is another story, and one that, it occurs to me now, might well bespeak the difference between synchronization and synchonicity.

There is, after all, more to meaningful coincidence than simply being in the same place at the same time. In addition to being coincidental it also has to be meaningful. But clearly, what's meaningful to one person might be meaningless to someone else. "Meaning," therefore, only has meaning on a personal level. An event becomes meaningful for someone when a connection is sensed between his inner and outer world, her subjective and objective reality. Which suggests that a whole lot of potentially meaningful stuff could be going unnoticed, and that if we could but pay closer attention, or sense greater connection, then the world would take on greater meaning.

With synchronicity, the connection often shows up as a forethought or a prescient vision.

Some people put a lot of energy into trying to figure out how to increase the frequency of those thoughts and visions. Perhaps the example of thieves and musicians provides us with a clue. By setting our watches to the same time and tuning our instruments to the same frequency, we increase the likelihood of being together in time. Only in this case we're using hearts and minds rather than watches and guitars.

And while Greenwich Mean Time might seem like something special on earth, when we get to talking universe, and about being in synch with the universe, we have to consider things from the perspective of eternity, or the eternal now, which are the same, and ever-present and never-ending. As for which frequency to tune to, keep in mind the concept of resonance, and how a "force" vibrating at a particular frequency can cause another object tuned to that same frequency to start vibrating too. Which is why, if you're looking for trouble you're likely to find it, and why a sure way to spread peace is by being peaceful.

June 4, 2001

Changing routines, changing motion

Today at lunch, a friend of mine was questioning whether he had any willpower at all left.

"I don't think I can say no anymore, if I want something," he said.

I told him about a little trick I do that involves breaking the routine.

It doesn't matter what the routine is. Say it's waking up and, first thing, having a cup of coffee. Maybe, just to change things up, you can put the coffee off for two or three hours. Or replace it with something else. Or maybe it's coming home from work and flicking on the TV to watch the evening news. Instead, to change things up, you could pop in a favorite music CD, or read a book, or go sit outside on the driveway with your baby and discuss your day, or your dreams, or your disappointments.

It works wonders, because when you see yourself starting to take control over one thing, even a little thing, then you start to gain a bit of confidence that you can control something else. And then one thing leads to another, and pretty soon you start getting the notion that you can do something about the things that are important to you.

I remember one time, I was in the midst of a few-year plan to gain greater control over my emotions, and it occurred to me that if I was really serious about developing my will and gaining control then I might as well start with something as simple as what I put in my mouth. So I decided that for one year I would not eat any meat, or dairy, or sugar, and I wouldn't drink any alcohol or coffee. And I didn't, for 365 days. On the 366th day, I went to this little Mexican restaurant on campus and ordered the biggest, gooiest, meatiest, cheesiest burrito they had, and I drank a cerveza or three. And the next morning I went to, what would become, my favorite coffee shop, and ordered a fresh-brewed bean beverage and a bodacious bakery treat.

Some people wondered – why start up again, but my feeling was why not? It was never a matter of me thinking those things were "bad." It was just a matter of needing to know I could control what went into my mouth before I felt like I could make any real progress in regards to what came out of my mouth. And, as far as I can tell, it worked. It helped me stop feeling sorry for myself and verbalize far fewer negative expressions.

Not that I don't slip back into it from time to time. After all, self-awareness and the control of our being is not like riding a bike, where once you know how to do it you never forget. Although, I imagine, once you get to the top levels of competitive cycling, there are some days and races where it seems like you've forgotten how to do it. My point, though, is just because you're able to control your talk, or your diet, or your habits and addictions one day doesn't mean that you've got it mastered forever and ever.

Sure, the hope is that any effort you put in will pay off and lead to greater control, and that the "times away" from your graceful soul, your loving heart and your understanding mind get less and less, both in terms of frequency and duration. But the reality is that there is not one among us who doesn't "fall from grace" now and then. Everyone here has done or said something he wishes he could take back; or has forgotten something, or reacted to something, or lost control somewhere along the line.

It's an on-going battle.

In the inner battles, just as in some of the outer battles, it's not always best to approach it head on. Sometimes it works

better to sneak around the other side and mount a surprise attack. And that's what this routine-breaking stuff is about. You
go to where you're not expected and where you don't appear to
pose a threat.

For instance, if your sluggish self is on the lookout for someone or some part of you that's going to try and tell it to eat and
drink a little less and work out a little more, then, if and when it
spots such an accuser it'll likely resist. There's a chance, though,
that it might not even take notice of someone who comes along
and tells it to set the alarm clock a half-four earlier, or to get out
of bed on the other side, or to drive a different route to work.
And in this way, you can very quietly set some changes in motion.

And that's really what it comes down to, a study of motion;
a consideration of forces; momentum and inertia. Which is why
Newton has a place in every personal growth and development
library.

June 12, 2001

To try and achieve the love we conceive

What are you doing," asked the voice on the other end, when I picked up the ringing telephone.

I knew who it was, but I acted like I didn't because a) it was way too early for the phone to be ringing and I didn't want the person to think that it was perfectly all right to be disturbing my household at such an hour, and; b) because I didn't want to reinforce the notion that we're really close friends. If we were, mind you, then it would be O.K. to call anytime. Or even if we weren't good friends, but managed to have good talks, or exchange good vibes, or something. But that isn't the case. It's just, I don't know, something left over from another time and place; the vestiges of a gang of strangers in a strange land.

I could tell by the slur in her voice that she was smashed, as she has been every single time she's phoned me over the past seven or so years.

It's almost always the same thing – a fight with her boyfriend. And she goes on talking about what an oppressive jerk he is, and what a misunderstood and unfortunate thing she is, and she always gets around to how every man who walks the earth desires her and how she deals with that. For a while there, I'd stay on the phone with her for hours at a time, trying to listen, and let her know that there are people who care, and who recognize her talents and inner qualities. But then, a few times, she started badmouthing the guy, obviously right in front of him, and he grabbed the phone out of her hand and started yelling at me that I had no clue what he was having to deal with in dealing with her. And I've never even met the guy. And I certainly didn't want to be in the middle of something like that, so I just backed way way off. And from there, it just became more and more of a drag every time she'd call.

So, this time she called, it took about a minute for her to start complaining that I never call her, and she said, "don't you understand, I love you and I need to hear from you once in a while." Well, I wasn't about to bite on that, neither with "an I love you too," or a promise of "I'll call you," because I knew I wouldn't. I've never even written down her phone number. So I just sat there saying nothing at all. But she persisted, saying it over and over in all different kinds of ways, and adding, "even if you never ever call me, I'll still go on calling you because I love you."

She wasn't talking about romantic love, she was talking about friendship love. And the more she said it, the more I resisted giving her even the tiniest indication that I would ever call her, but she finally did pull out of me a "look, I love you too." What I meant by it was, "when it comes down to it, I really do care about you," but upon saying it, I had to ask myself, "what does that really mean, and what does it obligate me to?" And I went on asking myself those questions for the next few days.

Clearly, there are different kinds of love. There's the love between lovers, the love of family and friends, love of work, of play, of place. There's all-time love, and sometime love, full-time love and part-time love. Whichever love one may care to consider, the idea is the same – that talk is cheap, and that just saying it doesn't mean diddly-squat.

I've often felt that the meaning of the word, when spoken one-on-one, has been diminished through overuse. At the same time, I use it, and feel it, a lot, and with a lot of different people.

The phone call was but a reminder, and may it be a reminder, to keep asking and answering what it means to say, "I love you." And, from there, to set out loving. To aspire to love. To try and achieve the love we conceive. And to conceive of ever-greater meanings of love.

And while our conceptions may differ, one thing we can all be fairly certain of is that the way of love focuses more on giving than getting. It knows it is in giving that we get, and that we get what we give. For that is the law. As mathematically just, wrote Emerson, as the two sides of an algebraic equation.

June 25, 2001

Spread the word,
spread the goosebumps

After several days of scorching heat, I knew, upon waking, that the day would be a blessing. It was cool and cloudy, and before long, it was raining. And then the next thing I knew, I was out dancing in the rain. Jubilantly twirling around with arms out and face skyward, sending out my thanks and praise for the large-scale and deep-felt refreshment.

A great big raindrop plopped smack dab on my forehead, which I must say is not some great rarity considering how much forehead I have, and it sent a chill though my body. It shivered me timbers and sent goosebumps rippling through my body. It occurred to me what a strange and wonderful phenomena goosebumps are.

What are goosebumps, I asked myself, and after more than an hour of searching through dictionaries, encyclopedias, and online reference sites, all I came up with is that a muscle underneath the skin called the erector pilli, contracts and makes your hair stand up, thus, giving you, what is commonly known as, goosebumps. But there's more to it, I protested, than just the hair standing up, there's the actual bumps that pop out all over the place. Some people call them goose pimples, others call it chicken flesh, and my friends from Spain call it "sea urchin." I know there has to be a technical term for the phenomenon of which I speak, but darned if I could find it. Not that it matters, for far more interesting to me than what the real name of goosebumps is, and more interesting, too, than what the name of the muscle is that contracts to produce goosebumps, is what causes that muscle to contract.

Clearly, there are all sorts of things that cause people to get goosebumps. I'm not so much interested in the physical causes, like being cold, for instance, although, I'm always more than happy to think about my baby's light and loving touch, which does it to me, and does it to me good. That sensation of being right on the edge between being tickled and being soothed is a place I like to hang out.

Synchronicity gives me goosebumps. Like, for instance, when someone's on your mind, and then that someone calls, seemingly out of the blue. Or when you're thinking about something, and then someone comes along and starts talking about the exact thing you're thinking about. Or when you miss your exit on the freeway, and then later find out that an accident had occurred right where you were supposed to get off. Those kinds of things give me goosebumps.

So does watching the awards ceremonies in the Olympics. Seeing the person up there on the platform as the flag is being raised. Knowing the work and training that went into it, and seeing the faces on the family and friends who have been there and watched every step of the way as the whole thing developed and unfolded. Recognizing the grand achievement, in a moment of recapitulation – that makes me shudder.

And a good performance of a good song can do it for me. Usually it happens in live performance, but sometimes a recording can cause it to happen as well. I could, I'm sure, fill up several pages just listing the songs and artists and performances that have given me goosebumps along the way. When I pressed myself, though, to remember actual times it has happened, both live and on record, the first examples that came to mind were performances by The Band of "It Makes No Difference" and Santana's recording of "Samba Pa Ti," respectively. And then I thought of Willie Nelson performing "Angel Flying Too Close to the Ground," and the Beach Boys' recording of "In My Room."

And speaking of The Beach Boys, we got a phone call the other day from a friend telling us to turn on the television because there was a program on paying tribute to Brian Wilson. The funny thing is, not more than 10 minutes earlier I had been speaking to my baby about The Beach Boys. So we flicked on the tube, and switched to the show, just in time to see our friend and neighbor, David Crosby, join Carly Simon and Jimmy Webb in a rendition of, you got it, "In My Room."

After listening to the likes of Elton John and Billy Joel sing other Brian Wilson songs, I then watched with great interest as George Martin, the great producer and the co-creator of The Beatles' music, got up and paid his humblest and highest respects for Brian Wilson's work in the recording studio. He stated that Brian Wilson combined the songwriting talents of John and Paul, the performing abilities of George and Ringo, and his own production skills, all rolled into one. He spoke of how The Beatles were inspired by Brian, and he guessed that if Mozart had been alive in the 1960s that he would have probably spent most of his time working in a recording studio competing with Brian Wilson. And hearing those things come out of his mouth, him being who he is, well, it gave me goosebumps.

I know some people judge and evaluate music by whether or not it gets their toes tapping and their body moving. My love for dance notwithstanding, I'm much more turned on by music that gives me goosebumps.

So while I have, on occasion, been known to put forth an admonishment to spread the word, or to spread the light, this week, I think I shall say "spread the goosebumps."

July 8, 2001

Feel what you look like,
See what you feel like

I picked up our roll of pictures, and tore open the envelope, anxious to see the record of the previous day's big adventure. But when I pulled them out and started shuffling through, it shocked me. It literally freaked me out to see these pictures of myself because they look so different than the image I carry around in my mind.

It's hard for me to understand how this can be, because it's not like I don't look at myself in a mirror occasionally. Maybe it's like Paul Simon said, when he wrote: *"A man sees what he wants to see and disregards the rest."* Which, I suppose, in my case could mean that I see the freedom of spirit I feel inside, the passion and romance that are so much a part of my work and home, and the beauty and excitement I have found along the way, while at the same time, disregarding the lines on my face, the tiredness in my eyes, the thinning hair and the widening body. I don't know, maybe, maybe not.

I think my confusion has to do with the fact that I feel pretty confident in most situations, and then I look at these photos, and I think — a guy who looks like that has no business feeling so confident. I'm kidding, of course, for I know that my confidence doesn't stem from, and has nothing to do with, my physical appearance. It never did. I know too, for I witness it day in and day out, time and time again, that beauty is truly in the eye of the beholder. Which makes me so grateful to have so many beautiful people around me who see me through their beautiful eyes.

And while it still seems extremely bizarre to me for a normal-sighted adult human being to be so far off the mark as far as knowing what he looks like, nevertheless, my sense of what's what tells me that it's more important to know what you look like on the inside than on the outside. For that I look into a different kind of mirror — the mirror of the soul.

In meditation and contemplation, I take a blank slate and draw a vertical line down the middle. On the one side I list, or call to mind, what I consider to be my virtues, and on the other side, I catalog my shortcomings, the goal being to systematically increase the number of entries on the virtue side, and to reduce the number of faults on the downside. Of course, just saying it or wishing it doesn't make it so. It involves much work on being, but that's another topic for another time.

I always thought, though, that by doing this, by gazing earnestly into the mirror of my soul, I could remain fairly honest with myself. But after this latest photo-contradiction, it makes me wonder, if it's so easy to fool myself when visual evidence is readily available, might it not be even easier to be deceived where and when the evidence is not quite as easy to come by. And the answer is, yes, of course, for we all deceive ourselves, much and many times more than others deceive us.

Bruce Lee, whom many people know or think of only as a martial artist and a movie star, but whom I think of as a master of living, suggested that we see ourselves most clearly in the mirror of relationship.

"To know oneself," wrote Lee, *"is to study oneself in action with another person. Understanding comes about through feeling, from moment to moment in the mirror of relationship."*

I love that; not *looking* in the mirror, but *feeling* in the mirror.

You observe how what others do and say makes you feel, and how what you do and say makes others feel, and in that way you get a picture of who you are and how you are; how weak and strong you are; how lively or how listless you are; if you're a giver or a taker, and if you have a sense of humor. It's those sorts of qualities, much more so than height, weight, hair color, eye color or skin color, that describe a person, or get across the idea of what's unique about someone

We've all heard the term "two-way" mirrors. They are devices that from one direction reflect the image back at you but from another vantage-point allow you to see clear through to the other side. Well, that's exactly the kind of thing that is needed to help us feel what we look like and see what we feel like.

As for the guy in the photographs who I hardly even recognize, I'm reminded of Camelback Mountain in Phoenix. Driving on the one side of the mountain, it looks just like a camel with a little praying monk walking up its nose. From the other side, though, it doesn't look anything like that. It's the same thing with the photos. That might be how I look from where the camera was, given the particular lighting conditions, but you should see how I look from this side.

July 11, 2001

Participation in the perpetuation of myths

Even if our models of the universe, and the laws of cause and effect, are mathematically precise, the world of humans isn't. And there is no one I know who can say, unequivocally, here's what's what and this is the way things are. And yet, I've run into at least three people in the last week alone who ended up getting discouraged by someone saying to them, in effect, "this is the way things are." And them buying it.

In saying so, the person doing the talking was putting forth a pronouncement that "what you're doing doesn't have value, and no one's interested in it." And rather than using it as fuel for the fire, the people it was told to used it as a reason to change their plans, if not also their minds and hearts.

All three cases involved people in the music business, and the comment that was made, in each case, was "the only thing that sells is hip-hop;" referring to the currently popular style of music. My personal feelings aside, as to whether it should even be called music, I know this is not a true statement, only because I've bought at least 20 new CDs this year, and none of them are what you would call "hip-hop." And I've got a bunch of friends all over the country, and we like to turn each other on to the music that's turning us on, and nothing that has come my way from the others falls into the "hip-hop" category. So I know *something* besides hip-hop is selling to *someone.*

I know, too, that it's a matter of a scale; mega-millions versus however-many thousands.

One of the questions I keep asking, though, is how is something going to sell if you're not selling it?" All you need to do is turn on the television to see that what they're selling is "hip-hop." They're selling it on the radio stations, in the clothing stores, at the football and basketball games, at the movies and in the video games.

It brings to mind a little story of when my nephew was about two years old, and my sister said, "The only thing he'll eat is avocados." And my dad was like, "He's two years old. If that's what you feed him, that's what he'll eat."

The difference here is that, unlike the two-year-old, if we don't like what's being served then going somewhere else to eat is, maybe, a possibility.

One of the things I've learned along the way, by dining out in places like Paris, Florence, and even places as unlikely as Anaheim, is that better price, better taste, and most likely a better experience too exist just a few blocks away, off of the main drag.

As for this attitude that there's only room for the biggest selling stuff, I'm compelled to ask what's wrong with however-many thousands if it's still making money, if it's not losing money? Some might argue that spending money on a "style" of music that might only net you six figures, when you can spend it on hip-hop, or something else altogether that might make you nine figures is money misspent. But what kind of a world would it be if there were only room for the giant sequoias and not the poplars; only the elephants and not the guinea pigs; the oceans but not the lakes, cities but no towns?

Those who spout out such all-encompassing claims, such as, "hip-hop is the only thing that sells," would have us believe those things, but we who live in towns and walk among the poplars know otherwise.

Surely we have learned by now that quantity is no measure

of cool, and not a very good one of quality either.

And I'm not so sure if I'm wanting to direct my comments now more to the "business-people" who are saying these kinds of things, to the music people who are getting it told to them, or to anyone at all who accepts such stuff. The line, though, that comes to my mind is the Pink Floyd lyric that goes, "*All in all, you're just another brick in the wall.*"

If you don't buy it, or if you'd rather it not be that way then don't participate in the perpetuation of the myth. Don't withhold your gifts, your contributions, just because you're not sure if someone else is going to recognize the value in them, and neither render yourself powerless by focusing on the uncertainty of the future rather than the fulfillingness of the present. It's journey versus destination stuff, doing it because that's what comes from your heart not because that's what's selling.

Being *yourself* is *your* virtue; thinking your thoughts, feeling your feelings, and adding your little piece of the puzzle, your part of the magnificent whole.

Just as it is the virtue of the knife to cut, likewise it is the virtue of the musician to make music. Take on the challenge of virtue.

It's time to quit asking permission to be who and what we are. If you believe morals and courage are needed then refrain from making (or believing in) demoralizing statements and discouraging remarks.

July 16, 2001

Call it new,
but there's nothing new about it

And so now, some British scientist says he has evidence that would seem to suggest that consciousness continues after the heart and brain have stopped functioning and the person is dead.

He says this based on a study of people who were officially pronounced dead but then later revived. Some of them, he says, report having lucid memories of thinking, reasoning, moving about and communicating with others after doctors determined their brains were not functioning.

And I'm like, O.K., but this is nothing new. People have been telling me about this stuff since before I first left my parents' house, which has been a while now, and writing about it for thousands of years.

Consciousness which is supraphysical; metaphysical; more powerful than physical.

It's hard for me to imagine - except in cases involving brain damage or other bodily illness or injury, which may have impeded ordinary, or at least typical, human relations, associations, and exchange of information - anyone over 40 years old not having been exposed to the same sort of stuff, regardless of the words, titles, names and qualities used to describe it. And since the majority of people alive on the planet today are older than 40, and since many of them have already taught it to their kids, that means, or at least I'm guessing, most people have already been exposed to this.

But here it is, being announced on the news and in the science magazine, like it's some brand new thing. And I'm wondering, what, did all these people just disregard it? Do they not believe it? Did they ever believe it? And if not, why not?

I surely don't claim to know what anyone else thinks or believes, but according to this scientist, the reports that have come out of near-death experiences have been, for the most part, ignored by the scientific community, and attributed to oxygen deprivation. In other words, all the stories of intense peacefulness, of bright light, of time speeding up, of watching your own body from above, are said to be but the effects of the brain playing tricks on the mind, or the mind playing tricks on itself. Explanations that would seek to reduce the mystery.

And while I can certainly appreciate critical thinking, and the confidence and independence that is needed to not just blindly accept whatever gets told to you, it can get rather aggravating, can't it, dealing with people who flat-out refuse to accept anything which cannot be measured on a scale, or with a watch or a ruler, or somehow similarly quantified?

And then there are those whose need to provide proof is just as strong and rigid as the skeptics' need to be provided with proof.

They both remind me of the story of the "doubting Thomas," the apostle who, when told by his cohorts of the great resurrection, said, in essence, "I ain't buying it. Not unless I can see His hand with nail holes in it, and stick my finger through there, and put my hand on His body. Not without those things am I willing to believe it."

And then, once he did see and do those things, he believed it all the way, and he went out and spread the word. All through India, say some. And he was even killed for it, that's how much he believed, and how much he walked the talk. But the point, as it was told to him, was that it took him seeing before he believed. "Blessed," said the Lord, "are they that have not seen, and have believed."

Gullibility is one thing, and blind faith something else, but it is a virtue to be able to believe in that which cannot be seen

I suppose if this sort of scientific pronouncement helps people accept that there is a force or presence within us that transcends the usual physical limitations, and the normal human ups and downs, and if that acceptance gets people paying a little more attention to it, then great. But the soul needs no such verification.

It's kind of like Columbus discovering America. Maybe that "discovery" helped the Europeans believe that there was a new world out there, but for the people already inhabiting that world, there was nothing new about it. And for us, there's nothing new in the idea that there is more to it than meets the eye.

As for people not paying attention to it, it reminds me of the Sufi story about the dervish and the scholar who struck up a conversation on board a ship while crossing the channel.

"Have you ever read the classics," asked the scholar.

When the dervish answered, no, he hadn't, the scholar said, "Then half of your life has been wasted."

A while later, the dervish turned to the scholar and asked him if he had ever learned to swim. The scholar said he hadn't, to which the dervish replied, "Then all of your life has been wasted. We're sinking."

July 3, 2001

She's the birthday girl and the gift

This might not be the right place for this, but it just seems a bit weird to me for me to write about anything other than my daughter on this her second birthday. And yet, what can I say about it being her birthday? That time flies and it seems like only yesterday that she was born? Everyone else is saying that for me. But though the day and night-before she was born are still so close at hand, when I stop to consider it, and connect then to now, it feels like two years; two *full* years.

Looking at her wearing and playing with her new gifts, I ponder the gifts she gives me, daily.

Like **enthusiasm**; the kind she just ran through the room with, while exclaiming, "the moon, the moon!" She expresses that same kind of enthusiasm every time she finds something that she hasn't seen for a few days; like her bike, an old slipper or the plastic bottle with Big Bird on it. The same kind of excitement that comes bursting out each time she recalls the car-wash, pink skies, the beach and the zoo.

She gives the gift of **music** by making music a gift. Whenever it comes on, either on the radio in the car, on the TV or stereo or her little CD player, and now at the Thursday concerts, she jumps up and gets into it. And because she loves listening to it, we make sure to have it playing. And, of course, we're only going to have music on that we like, so that's one way she gives us the gift of music. Another way is that she *plays* music all the time, and it's completely entertaining to watch her when she blows harmonica, or plays the tambourine, or beats rhythm with spoons and forks on pots or a table-top. She likes to strum the guitar too, which prompts me to pull it out every so often. And when I do, I play and sing a few, which is yet another way she gives the gift of music. And she loves to dance, and she knows several different dances. There's the one she does where she goes around in circles, the one where she pumps her arms up and down, and the one where she bends over and touches the ground, and sometimes even gets all the way down until she's lying flat on her back.

Politeness is another of the gifts she brings. She's so danged polite. Obviously, we're the ones, along with her extended circle, that had to teach it to her, but she drew it out of us. She is at least as consistent with her pleases and thank-yous as we are, which keeps us there too.

She also brings this incredible gift, or perhaps it would be better to call it a love, of **learning**. Whenever we make a point of teaching her something, she wants to know more. Books are her favorite toys, and she loves to be quizzed. At two, she knows the alphabet, both looks-wise and phonetically, she knows right and left, is pretty good with the days of the week, and knows who's daddy's mother, poppa's son, mommy's sister, auntie's daughter, uncle's wife and cousin's pet. I had one woman jump all over me in the store when, upon my seeing her name printed on a sign, I pointed and asked her, what letter is that? You shouldn't be asking her that kind of stuff until she's seven, said this woman. She should be playing and having fun, to which I said, she has fun *and* she knows her "F." It has nothing to do with what or how we want her to be, nor with us pushing her; she's pushing us to teach her more that she might learn more, and communicate more. Following her lead, I'm petitioning Life to teach me more that I might learn and communicate more.

And there's the gift of **affection** she brings to and out of us; her hugs and kisses, and her pleas for the same. Even in this rush-a-day world, she keeps us cognizant of the fact that there's always time enough for those things.

I could go on all night about the things she does and says, and maybe it's a good time for me to write some of that stuff down, but to complete this "perspective" on my daughter turning two years old, I'll just say that while this age and time period we are now entering is often referred to as "the terrible twos," these past 730 days, Scottsdale, Region One and yesterday notwithstanding, have been, in the words of the late Lawrence Welk, whom my grandmother called, Lorenza Velka, "wunaful, wunaful."

Since day one, when her heart was beating but she wasn't breathing, she has been a paradox. She remains so to this day. For though she may be the birthday girl, from where I'm standing, she is also the gift.

July 31, 2001

The meaning of words
and the energy of expression

Sometimes it takes someone coming in from out of town to get us to go out and see some of the sights and attractions of the place we live. Likewise, sometimes, it takes someone learning English as a Second Language to teach those of us whose first language it is the meaning of certain words. Such was the case today when our Spanish-speaking friends bestowed a compliment upon our daughter. But even though we were familiar with the word, we didn't think it was a compliment. Luckily, we're good enough friends with them to not feel weird about it, and we discussed the word and their usage of it, and eventually looked it up. But not in a dictionary, we looked it up in their vocabulary-enhancement book that goes along with their vocabulary-enhancement tape. And when we heard the definition, we realized it was a compliment after all.

It shocked us when we found out that's what the word meant, and, just to make sure, we looked it up in our own dictionary. Sure enough, their understanding of the word was correct and ours wasn't.

They then proceeded to quiz us on a bunch of the other words in their book. We knew most of them, but there were some we didn't know. The discouraging part of it is that they're only at the first level of their learning program. We weren't discouraged, though, for it struck us that probably 80 percent of the people we interact with would probably never use 80 percent of the words from that book in a sentence.

At first I wondered whether it was representative of how illiterate we have become, in general.

For instance, most of the people in this country have never read a book. One of the beauties of reading is that we get introduced to different words and different use of the language. When we don't read, our vocabulary stagnates. Worse, it diminishes. Next thing you know, different people are using the same word to describe different qualities. Like awesome, for instance. Around where I live, everything's awesome. An awesome meal, an awesome ride, an awesome song, and an awesome heater, dude. The same word used to describe that which is delicious, thrilling, engaging and effective.

Not that I mind, mind you. I love, and love using, the word awesome. My dictionary defines this word as "inspiring awe," and "expressive of awe." Awe is defined as "overwhelming wonderment combined with fear or reverence." Wonderment and reverence are among the states of mind and heart I aspire to, so if using the word as much as I do indicates that different sights and sounds and sensations are able to produce such feelings in me, then I shall gladly go on using it in myriad situations.

Which brings me to my next point — that the dwindling of our language could be a sign that we are becoming more direct and to the point in our communication.

Consider that when we were still primitive, our verbal communication consisted of grunts and groans, gestures and gesticulations to express feelings, desires and warnings. Gradually, as language developed, we started pronouncing words, and with more words came the ability to get across ideas, and convey concepts. Our intellectual understanding blossomed. But somewhere along the line, the growing mind meant less room for the heart. We pursued knowledge while disregarding wisdom. We sought justice while lacking compassion. We let our ideas out but kept our feelings in. We gathered evidence, and lost faith.

Maybe now, the pendulum is swinging back the other way. Maybe now it's the heart that's expanding.

Not that the heart and the mind can't grow together. As a matter of fact, our harmonious development depends on it. But maybe the quality of communication, in this day and age, is determined less by our eloquence and more by our passion.

Which is not to condone illiteracy. It's just to point out that despite the power and beauty of language, still, sometimes, we express ourselves more through our energy than our vocabulary.

"Discretion of speech is more than eloquence; and to speak agreeably to him with whom we deal is more than to speak in good words, in good order."

– Francis Bacon

"Energy of mind, genius, power, wherever it exists, may speak out in any tongue, and the world will hear it."

– Daniel Webster

He who combines energy and eloquence has the capacity to stir our hearts and enlighten our minds.

August 28, 2001

Conventional wisdom changes over time

When I was in high school, they told us that you shouldn't lift weights for baseball or basketball because it will shorten your muscles and limit your range of motion. Nowadays, you see these NBA players with incredible physiques, obviously developed through weight training, and you've got baseball players hitting more homeruns than ever before, and many of them are attributing it to strength gains brought on by working with weights. They've found that weight-training not only makes you stronger, it makes you faster, it improves your balance, it builds your endurance, it prevents injuries, and, in the event that an injury should occur, it speeds up your recovery time. As a result, weight-training has made it, literally, a whole new ballgame.

Or, consider the kitchen and the dining room. It seems like it wasn't all that long ago that pasta was good for you and wine was bad for you, and now it's pasta's bad for you and wine is good for you.

The point is, conventional wisdom changes over time.

My friend must have been thinking along these same lines today when he was talking about how, "They used to tell you, 'Keep your business and your personal life separate. Then, what ended up happening was, you had all these people with split personalities."

He was talking about the process of becoming comfortable, at peace even, with himself and his body. In his case, once he knew for sure who and what he was, he no longer saw any point in spending any part of his day, which meant a part of his life, being someone he's not, and doesn't want to be.

It brings to mind something that happened to me, long long ago, when I was a young boy. I was always a top student, but never THEE top student. So one day, the math teacher gives this problem to us out loud, and says raise your hand when you've got the answer. I went through my computations, came up with an answer, and raised my hand. As the first one to come up with the solution, the teacher called on me to give my answer. As I was drawing in breath to make my grand announcement, my eyes darted over to the desk next to me, which was occupied by THEE top student, and I noticed his answer, which was different than mine, and in that moment I had a decision to make. Do I say the answer that I came up with, or do I say the one that the smartest guy in the class came up with? I had only a fraction of a second to decide, and then I said it – his answer. As it turned out, it was wrong ... and mine was right. It was such a bummer, not only to be wrong in public, but to be wrong with someone else's answer, especially when I knew that I had the right answer. But what could I say – "No, really, I got it right, it's just that I cheated off a guy who got it wrong?" So I had to live with the knowledge that I had plenty enough smarts to come up with the right answer, and to come up with it first, but not enough confidence in myself to proclaim it.

I decided right then and there that life is too short to not be present and accountable in the time and space that you occupy, and opportunity is too precious to squander. I realized that we are each these unique and wonderful beings, and are each responsible for adding our own special little piece of the puzzle. We each have our own road to hoe, our own cross to bear, our own truth to arrive at, and the sum total of each of our contributions and experiences make up the incredible configuration that is the collective consciousness. If we forsake the responsibility of our uniqueness, and renounce the reality of our inter-dependence, then we limit our own and each other's awareness. If you go around in this world not being you, then you're no one. In which case, being with, or having, you, whether it's at a job, or in a relationship, is like being with or having no one.

Some people prefer it that way. They have as their aim to not make waves, to not disturb things, to leave things just as they found them, so they come and go quietly, unassumingly. It's a stoic approach.

Others want to leave something in their wake, they want to make a difference, perhaps make the world a better place. It's a heroic approach.

The hero's challenge, now, as it has always been, is to arrive at the truth and the totality of who you are, and to bring yourself to the table, to the task, to the time that is at hand.

In the old system of accounting and assessment, you pay close attention to how much you give and how much you get, but according to the guiding principles of spirit, you give all that you have and get all that you need. Conventional wisdom might say keep your business and your personal life separate, but the new wisdom says bring yourself unto all that you do and save yourself the pain of separation.

August 30, 2001

Responding to the 9-1-1 call

The ringing telephone woke us from our sleep. As Kelly climbed across to answer it, I pulled the pillow back and looked at the clock to see that it was 6 a.m.. Usually, the phone ringing that early in the morning means there's some kind of horse emergency going on in the barn, but this time it wasn't that. Kelly moved the phone away from her mouth to inform me that a plane had just crashed into the World Trade Center.

What in the heck is someone doing calling us at this hour to tell us that, I wondered. A minute or two later, with her still on the phone and listening to the caller telling the story, she suddenly expressed greater alarm as she found out, and then told me, that a second plane crashed into the other giant tower at the World Trade Center.

Still more asleep than awake, I was picturing little twin-engine planes, or maybe commuter jets. I had no idea we could be talking about commercial jumbo jets. I also had no idea we were talking about jets that had been hijacked.

Kelly got out of bed first, and with our daughter, went to the couch and flicked on the news. By time I rolled out and joined them, reports were coming in of two other planes that had been hijacked, one of which had crashed into the Pentagon.

And suddenly, it became clear. America was under attack, and the financial and military centers of our nation were the primary targets. It left us wondering how much more we might be in store for throughout the day.

Over the next hour, we watched in disbelief and horror as the twin towers, the fifth and sixth tallest buildings in the world collapsed to the ground, and New Yorkers ran screaming though southern Manhattan.

"Everything's changed," I said. "We've moved into a whole new phase, and the rules are totally different."

Realizing the enormity of the events, I looked at my daughter, and remembered myself being not much older than her, feeling the dread and sadness in my family's home the day JFK died. She didn't seem to be aware of our misery.

After watching the same reports over and over again for a couple hours, I decided to take a shower. As I stepped into the tub, it felt strange to me to be going about my normal morning routine while thousands of people in our country were dying at the hands of terrorist attacks. Maybe I've read too many Tom Clancy novels, but I made a conscious decision to have a good and thorough shower because I didn't know when I might get another one.

As I stood there under the streaming spray of hot water, I thought of Lexington and Concord and "the shot heard 'round the world." I thought of the raid at Harper's Ferry, the attack on Fort Sumter and, of course, the bombing of Pearl Harbor; the names and places, the milestone events that pulled this nation into its wars. But in each of those cases, we knew who the enemies were, and in each case, the enemy was a country with a name, and a government with a headquarters. This time it was different because there was no "official" enemy to retaliate against.

As I stepped out of the shower and toweled myself dry, I found myself cursing my insurance agent for not having wrapped up the details on my life insurance policy. It wasn't that I thought I might die suddenly, but that some righteous "cause" might emerge that would seem worth dying for.

After getting dressed, I held my girls close, not wanting to let go. Kelly and I reinforced our heart and mind and soul connection so that even though we would be apart during the working day we would remain together and connected.

Throughout the day I prayed, alone and with others. I felt like I was on another planet or something, existing in a different gravitational field. I couldn't focus on affairs of business, nor did I want to, so I closed up shop and went home.

Don't ask me why, but as I was walking out to my truck, I started thinking about Muhammad Ali, and how he got thrown into jail in 1967 for refusing to go to Viet Nam. To paraphrase, he said, "I've got nothing against the Vietnamese." He pointed out a difference between a national enemy and a personal enemy.

It occurred to me that in this case the national and the personal enemy is once again, one and the same, and that that enemy is hatred. As I put the key in the ignition, I could hear Marvin Gaye singing, *"Only love can conquer hate."*

Earlier in the day, when we first started watching the news, Kelly made a point of noting the date – Sept. 11, but it wasn't until later that we realized that Sept. 11 is 9-11, the numerical symbol for an emergency call. The emergency is not ours, or New York's, alone, it is a world emergency. The call has been made, may we now come together to respond to this world emergency lovingly and effectively.

September 11, 2001

United 93; Remember the Alamo

Nine days later. The flags are still flying half-staff and it's still the only thing I can pull myself to write about.

This morning, and I don't remember if it was right before I went to bed in the early morning or shortly after I got up a few hours later, I started thinking about James Bowie and Davy Crockett. Names that are mythic in American folklore. But what do we know about them?

We know that James Bowie is the guy the Bowie knife was named after, and we know that Davy Crockett was a backwoods-frontiersman. And maybe we know that they both died at the Alamo.

(Just to give you an example of how "historical" information has come to me through song, I know Bowie and Crockett were both there due in no small part to the Jane Bowers song "Remember the Alamo," which I got introduced to through *the real Donovan* album. It says:

Jim Bowie lay dying, his blood and his powder were dry
But his knife had been ready to take him a few in reply
Young Davy Crockett lay laughing and dying,
the blood and the sweat in his eyes,
For Texas and freedom, a man was more willing to die"

Why do their names live on? What makes them heroes in our folklore? It's because they lived and died for freedom.

Bowie and Crockett were among that small group of Texans who, in 1836, held off 4,000 Mexicans at the Alamo in San Antone. Under the command of Colonel William Barrett Travis, the Texans held the mission for 12 days. Finally, there were no more of them left. They all died.

Throughout the rest of the war people held up their bravery

as an example, and reminded each other to "Remember the Alamo." People still say it. It's an admonishment to "remember those guys who never gave up, who fought to the death for freedom, and remember what we gained from it." It's also a challenge to "emulate that same level of commitment.")

It struck me that the crew and passengers of United Flight 93 can be held up as a similar example.

Consider that it was nearly two hours after the two planes crashed into the World Trade Center and an hour after another one crashed into the Pentagon. The passengers on those earlier planes responded to the hijackings in the way we have always been taught to – by remaining calm, and cooperating. But the passengers on UAL 93 knew that they weren't being whisked away to some location out of the country. They knew that they were a guided missile heading straight for some strategic target in the country, if not also straight at the unprotected heart of America. They weren't going to let that happen. At that moment, as my buddy over at the photo shop pointed out, there was a paradigm shift for how passengers might react in a hijacking. I would think also for how terrorists might think about hijackings. For it is a lot less glorious to kill a bunch of civilians going about their normal everyday non-violent lives then it is to bring down the Infidel, Capitalism and western culture.

One of the things that has always made these sorts of terrorists so frightening and dangerous is that they don't put a premium on human life. They believe they have a cause, and that it is noble, and they will go to any lengths in service to that cause. They'll gladly die for it because in their minds it makes them a hero and ensures them some big-time reward in the after-life. United 93 sends out a message that Americans too believe in a cause and are also willing to die for it. I imagine the enemy is more scared by that than by "we're coming at you with both guns blazing."

The people on that plane were protecting America. Their actions saved lives, and in all probability preserved the building that is the symbol of our way of government. That it remains standing is symbolic of our endurance. But what happened in New York verifies that our strength is not in our concrete structures but in our unbending resolve, and our greatness is not in our symbols but in the truths that stand behind those symbols. Let us be reminded that these are truths based on freedom, equality and fairness.

I'm guessing that the names Todd Beamer, Jeremy Glick, Thomas Burnett, and the others on the flight probably won't be remembered by anyone outside of their families or their immediate spheres of influence. Nevertheless, they deserve hero status on the level of Jim Bowie and Davy Crockett, and "United 93" is every bit as powerful and inspiring of a reminder as "Remember the Alamo."

September 20, 2001

Go ahead and change ... for the better

I hear all these newscasters and politicians telling us to get back to our normal routines, and to do exactly what we did before all this stuff happened because if we change what we do and how we live our lives then the terrorists will have won. Victory through disruption. I understand not giving up and not giving in, not caving in, not breaking down, not fearing, fretting or folding under pressure, but at the same time, there's a loud voice inside me going, "Forget that! Go ahead and change! Change for the better!"

I'm not talking about the kind of changes that involve getting on airplanes, or going to work or going shopping, or changing vacation plans or investment strategies or any other such outward considerations. The changes I'm referring to involve time and life, and the recognition of how precious they are.

People are here today and gone tomorrow, and once they're gone, that's it. Not to say that that's it, or to speculate on what happens to someone who passes on, only to emphasize that there will come a day when you won't be seeing that person around anymore, even though they may continue to dwell in your heart. You might begin to perceive them in different ways, maybe get impressions, receive messages, or even carry on conversations, but there won't be any more calling each other up on the telephone, or sitting together across the dinner table or over a cup of coffee. Which is why, it seems to me, we would all do well to consider how much of the limited time that we have together do we want to spend being irritated, not enjoying, complaining, bringing people down, or just generally being *part* of the problem? How much time do we want to spend reiterating what's wrong and how things are, as opposed to finding ways to make things different, and better?

And do we realize and remember that life comes to us *through* life, *from* life, and *only* from life? Inanimate objects made out of inorganic materials *do* not and *can* not instill life or make us alive. Only people can. Not only through the process of giving birth to biological life, but also through the exchange of the mysterious life-force that indwells all living things. Yet how often do we neglect people and living things because we happen to be preoccupied with other stuff? Material stuff, commercial enterprises.

Disregard of that sort cuts us off from each other, and makes us less sensitive, less understanding, and less wise. When we spend more time with each other, and pay more attention to each other, then we more fully observe each other going through life. We see it, and in doing so, we see that we all have our own way to go and each have our own lessons to learn. We become more accepting and less judgmental. We become greater respecters of life. Knowing that it is the supreme gift we squander it less, and appreciate it more.

We often hear the saying, "live each day as if it's your last," but how many of us actually do that? Instead, we put each other down, we put each other off, or otherwise put each other on hold. We get upset over little things. We do and say things that we probably wouldn't if we knew it was our last day, and we don't do and say other things that we probably would if we knew our time was about to run out. Well guess what, our time *is* about to run out. Whether it's a day, a week, a year, 50 years, or how ever long, our time is limited, and it is up to us to determine how much time we need to get at the truth of our lives and where we want to get to with each other.

Sometimes it takes something extreme happening for us to

see things in a different light – for us to remember how precious time is and how sacred life is. Perhaps this is one of those occasions and perhaps this is one of those times ... for us to change.

Oct. 1, 2001

Backward and forward;
the paradox and the challenge

I was listening in on a conversation today between two guys who make their living through the production and delivery of musical recordings, and one of them said, "The more sophisticated things get, the more you have to return to the basics."

Amen.

We have all these different technologies to improve our presentations and help us share information over great distances, either instantly or within a very short time, yet we still have tremendous difficulty communicating and there are far too many people who feel all alone.

I've got a friend who's quick to point out that when it comes to communication it's not so much the words you say as it is the feeling you say them with. The words may help you articulate your ideas but your demeanor conveys the way you feel about the person you're speaking with, as well as the subject you're speaking about and the situation you're speaking in. It answers a whole slew of questions that you might not even think to ask. While certain skills and devices might help you get your point across, attitudes, like actions, speak louder than words, imparting **not only that which you hope to reveal but also that which you cannot conceal.**

In physics, we speak of fields, such as the electric or the magnetic field. It describes a pattern or a condition that exists around an object. It represents a force, which is felt and experienced by other objects that come into the vicinity. Now instead of objects, let's talk about people and instead of fields let's talk about our presence.

It's the medium by which we make contact with each other ... the time and the space we occupy. That space, that time, exist right here, right now, in the present. Whatever else we may want to say about it, one thing's for sure, and that is **we can only be present in the present.**

I'm sure it wouldn't require much more than a moment's reflection for us to see and admit that often times, we are the ones responsible for keeping ourselves "out of" or "away from" the place-and-time in which we make contact with each other. This happens when we fix our attention on things not in the present. My masseuse says, "Where attention goes energy follows." If that's the case, then our energy is "going away" from the present, diminishing our presence, reducing the capacity and extent of our communication.

Another thing about the present, is that it's the place, or perhaps the time, where the past and the future meet and co-exist. The here and the now; the point of convergence for all that has been and ever shall be, and since we are never not in a spot or a situation where these two don't converge, it can be seen also as the point that eternity flows into and out of.

Some people like to speak of the old days. Others are forever heralding in the new age. Some people like to separate the one from the other. To choose one over the other, or to reject either, is to close ourselves off to half of everything that is possible. To remain in the awareness of the present is to place ourselves at the heart and center of all that is possible and impossible.

Each day, we are in a process of transitioning from the old to the new. But in the process of doing so we don't want to throw the baby out with the bath water. We want to hold on to our wisdom, and bring it with us. We want to be done with the thoughtlessness and carelessness that renders us fools. We want to be better, and have things around us be better too.

The key to making the transition and for moving from the old to the new is communication. But neither a higher tower, a bigger speaker nor a better computer will help us communicate more fully as long as the obstructions are not out there but rather in here, meaning within ourselves. Our biggest shortcoming is not a case of equipment, it is a matter of willingness and desire.

Robert Anton Wilson wrote, *"Communication is only possible between people who want to communicate."*

That's it. That's basic.

As my audiophile friends pointed out, it's time to get back to basics while simultaneously advancing forth into more highly developed innovation. To move forward and back at the same time is not only a paradox, it is our challenge.

October 6, 2001

Things to do and things to be

A friend and I were laughing about the "things to do list," and how it never gets done. It reminded me of Don Juan's comments on the mystery of life. He said that a warrior must strive ever to understand the immense and unfathomable mystery of life, while at the same time realizing that he has no hope of ever doing so. But still he must try.

Being a Buddhist, my friend commented on how the never-dwindling things-to-do list provides us with yet another opportunity to learn the lessons of forgiveness. I guess she was talking about not being hard on ourselves and each other for not accomplishing all that we want to within the time frame that we want to.

The next morning, I was awakened from my sleep, much earlier than usual, by further thoughts of the things-to-do list.

While I recognize its usefulness as an organizational tool, and while I realize, too, that big accomplishments are most often the result of a series of little accomplishments, it occurred to me that five years from now, we're not going to remember most of the things that nag at us today. We're not going to remember the details of these lists, or which items we crossed off and which ones we didn't. And since we're not going to remember them five years from now, that means that they're probably not all that important in the grand scheme of things. That's when I had the idea for a *things-to-be* list – not to replace the things-to-do but to be used along with it.

The things-to-do list is made up of tasks that are important for today, while the things-to-be list is made up of things that are important in the long run.

The things-to-be list begins with a good honest look in the

mirror. It arises out of going – *this* is how I am and *this* is how I want to be, and it evolves out of our efforts to paint a portrait of the person we want to become. For instance, you might, one day, take a look at yourself and notice, "I'm pretty edgy and short-tempered," and you might decide, "I would like to be calmer and more patient." Some people go as far as the looking part but they don't get to the painting part. They recognize how they are but they explain it with, "I'm that way because of this or because of that," which is really just another way of saying, "I'm not going to change until or unless this or that thing changes." Even if this is not *how* I want to be. It's a matter of accountability. Using the things-to-be list, whether you call it that or not, involves taking that further step.

Those of us who use things-to-do lists refer to them often throughout the day so we can keep track of things, and check whether or not we're "on task." The things-to-be list can be used in the same way. By referring to it often, it can help us determine whether we are *becoming* the person we want to be.

As for what sorts of things one might add to the things-to-be list, obviously, that's going to depend on one's personal outlook and values. One person may think that it's important to be nice, or fair, or to have a sense of humor, while those things may not even be a consideration for someone else. It's clear, though, that some things don't belong on a things-to-be list. For example, being well-dressed. Yes, you can *be* well-dressed, but that's not part of your being-ness. Whereas, something like elegance is. There are some people who are elegant no matter what kinds of clothes they wear. In thinking about the difference, I'm reminded of a lesson from Spanish class that has to do with when to use the word "es" and when to use the word "esta." "Es" implies permanence, as in John is (es) a boy, whereas "esta" means it's only temporary – as in John is (esta) at the store. You can describe a person as kind, or funny, or quiet, and mean that the person is *always* that way, or that they're that way *today*. The things on the things-to-be list aspire to the use of the word "es."

On last thing and another great value about the things-to-be list is that it is an effective scale for weighing the relative importance of things. No matter how pressing or seemingly important the things on the things-to-do list seem, they're not as important as the things on the things-to-be list.

October 16, 2001

How do you write a hug?

Sometimes, there just ain't a whole lot you can say to make someone feel better. Like this afternoon, when my friend looked me squarely in the eyes, and said, "I'm feeling *so* old." I knew it wasn't just a nonchalant comment, because I could see he was hurting.

Fact of the matter is – he *is* growing old. He's been through lifetimes in this lifetime, and his body's been through the mill, and despite all the great quotes about wisdom or about fine wines getting better with age, there was, I knew, nothing I could say to relieve his aches or ease his agony. Nor was he *looking* for me to say anything. He was just getting it out, and sometimes that's all you want or all you need. Sometimes, that's all it takes for you to latch on to something to feel better about.

I know, from my own experience, when I come home after a hard day, a stressful day, and I see my gal standing in the kitchen, I just want to hold her and stand there for a while before we speak. I don't want questions, I don't want answers, I don't want to go round and round about things, I just want to be there together, in the custody of closeness and contact. It's not that I'm looking to indulge in misery, or for her to put up with me or vindicate me. It's more about what I'm *not* looking for, namely, an argument or a verbal challenge.

Not that we argue, we don't.

We do speak our minds, though, and we speak, also, from our hearts. We know, and are grateful, that words, especially the right word at the right time, can shed light upon a situation and give rise to reorientation. But we prefer conversation to debate, only because in debate you have "sides." One person takes one side and the other person takes another side. We prefer to be on the same side, together, even when our viewpoints or feelings about something differ. This inclination leaves us sitting on the tailgate, watching the sunset; sitting on the porch watching the stars; sitting on tree-stumps gazing at the fire. It finds us expressing ourselves without feeling the need to convince or convert each other.

And while it is strictly a matter of personal taste, my preferences are pretty much the same when it comes to words in the written form. I'm less interested in attempts to convince than attempts to convey, less engaged by argument than by testimonial, and less moved by analysis than by expression.

No doubt, a well-thought-out and clearly elucidated argument can be compelling. It can give you a different perspective on things, and even change your mind. But how often do you come across an argument that produces real changes in your heart? Not that it need be one or the other. For me, a song can do both; so can that hug in the kitchen.

It reminds me of the Sufi story that talks about the power of logic. A student who had been away studying at the university returns to his village and tells the religious teacher that he no longer feels inclined to operate on faith. "I've learned," says the student, "that by using the laws of logic, I can prove anything I want." At which point, the priest hauls off and punches the kid in the nose, and says, "Then prove that doesn't hurt."

When I'm hurting, or reeling, or sometimes when I'm just trying to work something out inside myself, I'd rather be accepted than judged, and I'd rather be hugged than critiqued. Being a believer in the Golden Rule I try to "do unto others as you would have them do unto you," and that includes in my writing.

But how do you write a hug?

I just try and do it in the same way that I would give a hug in any other situation. By opening myself up, putting my arms and energy around it, and then pulling it in close.

October 18, 2001

Special delivery from some unlikely messengers

This is going to probably sound strange to you. It sure was, and still is, strange to me. But here's what happened –

I had just gotten my daughter down to bed, and I was praying for a topic, calling out to God, or Spirit, or the Universe, to give me something to write about. I decided to lie down and relax and be quiet, thinking that maybe if I silenced all the surface noise it would make it easier to hear the inner voice. Within minutes, I found myself drifting into the most relaxed state I'd been in for months, and soon I heard these angelic voices singing. But it wasn't the voice of angels I was hearing, rather, it was Waylon Jennings, Jessi Colter and Kris Kristofferson.

What made it even stranger is that these are not singers I listen to. I don't have any records by any of them. I *like* Waylon, Jessi Colter – I couldn't name even one song that she sings, and Kris Kristofferson, as great of a songwriter as he is, as a singer, well, let's just say it's not necessarily what I would call a beautiful angelic voice. And yet, these are the three who showed up to deliver the message. And they sang the most surprisingly sweet, pure, *angelic* harmony I've ever heard.

Now, you may wonder, as I've wondered, how did and how do I know that it was Waylon Jennings, Jessi Colter and Kris Kristofferson. All I can say is that I knew, beyond the shadow of a doubt.

As I came out of my restful state, I asked myself, what was that all about? But I knew, just as surely as I knew who the singers were, what it was about. I had asked for a topic, and a topic had been given. And that topic was harmony. As for what I was supposed to make of it, that would have to wait, for I had become too restful, and I was drifting off to sleep.

The next morning, when I awoke, I tried to shrug the whole thing off and convince myself I still didn't have a topic to write about. What, I asked myself, am I supposed to do, say that I had a mystical experience that somehow involved Waylon Jennings, Jessi Colter and Kris Kistofferson? I put it off for a couple more days, sure that I would find something better and more meaningful to write about. And then I remembered that bit about how our prayers are *always* answered, it's just not always the answer we're looking for, or it doesn't always come in a form that we recognize. I also remembered the Michael On Fire lyric that goes, "*If the Spirit speaks then you don't ask why.*" So I decided to quit asking why, and just go ahead and write about harmony.

Despite my usual contention that the lessons of harmony are, perhaps, best learned by listening to Everly Brothers records, I, instead, regarded the topic from the standpoint of the multi-faceted individual, and successive levels of harmonious existence. Clearly, harmony within society and harmony in the home depend on harmony within the individual. To speak of harmony within the individual is to suggest that body, mind and spirit are working together and *not* working against each other, and *that* requires the simultaneous and balanced development of all of our aspects and faculties. No great revelation, just a reminder is all.

But that wasn't all, for in ruminating further upon the topic, I eventually did go pick out an Everly Brothers record. I put on side two of the vinyl album "The Everly Brothers' Best," which begins with the song "All I Have to Do is Dream," and as always happens whenever I hear the song on the radio, I sang along. I listened for and sang the one part (Don's) through one verse and the bridge, and then the other part (Phil's) the next time it came around. I'm not much of a singer, but I was able to do the part most of the way through. It occurred to me that that's the important thing. You don't have to be great and you don't have to sing loud, you just have to do your part.

It seems to me that in personal, private, professional and political spheres, we sometimes mistake harmony for being in unison. Being in unison is everybody singing the same note. When everybody sings the same note, there is no harmony. It takes people singing different notes for there to be harmony. Likewise, it takes people thinking and believing in different things in order for us to speak of any real social or group harmony. We all have our part to play, or sing, as the case may be, and it's when those parts come together in "correct" relation that harmony is created.

October 21, 2001

From the trip comes the message of the journey

Each sign, each sight, each town and city name brought another story to mind. Tales born from 35 years of traveling this highway, first for family vacations, then for wild schoolboy getaways, then for my work and now for hers. Always gathering more material for the telling, though nowadays, it seems, I mostly recall the episodes of old. The things that make the greatest impressions now, perhaps because I have some money in my pocket and a reliable vehicle to drive, are the abstract images of beauty, which I pray shall seep in, deep in, and forever unlock the magic of my heart and the marvels of the mind.

When I first started driving this road, or riding it I should say, for I was much too young to drive then, it was a route, which they now call "the historic route." Back then, you could cruise for maybe an hour or so, a little more once you got out West, and then you'd have to slow way down as it brought you into and through a town. You saw what the towns looked like, and you tasted the local food and the local flavor in little family-owned diners and gas station cafes.

As I think back on those early trips, it occurs to me that it isn't so much the things we did once we got to where we were going that remain with me, rather, the things we saw along the way.

And then came the Interstate, and it made the traveling a whole lot faster because it went around the towns. Since you didn't have to go in to the towns anymore, unless you needed gas, you didn't, and so, at least as far as the travelers go, many of those towns essentially disappeared and became nothing more than a name on a sign. Each stop along the way soon offered the same fast food and the same budget motels, which, in some cases out there on the fringe of the indefinite have been oh so appreciated, let me tell you. But what in earlier times had made each place unique and different began to evaporate and become alike and the same. Adventure and newness dissolved into safeness and familiarity. Convenience and uniformity became the rule, and the focus shifted from the journey to the destination.

Luckily, through most of my traveling, and again I attribute this in large part to the circumstances and the lack of resources, the emphasis has remained solidly on the journey, and thus, has engendered innumerable tales.

The great songwriter Bernie Taupin wrote, "*I thank the Lord for the people I have found.*" I echo that, but add, and for the stories too.

As I roll along this great highway through canyon country and among the mesas, the stories swirl; not necessarily tales of travel, but memories of moments with friends when the flat world rose up and came alive. Thanks to modern technology, I can phone those friends from my car and acknowledge those moments. Sentimental, I know, but it serves to strengthen the connection and the communication.

Those vital experiences are at the core of who we are. They dictate the way we respond to what comes along.

I'm reminded of a very significant little exchange that I had last summer with an old friend who was hurting and angry. I said something that happened to really get to him in a way that he felt he needed to get gotten. He looked surprised and wanted to know what compelled or equipped me to ask him what I asked him. We both knew it was all that I've been through. Just as all that any and everyone goes through shapes their response and

determines the quality of their journey.
 "Everyone along the way
 Helped to get you here today."
   - mi Fratello

As the sun sets in Yavapai county, I roll on westward, alone and in silence, on a day when we change the clocks to save an hour of light, which we will in turn give back in the spring. In this light, and in this hour, the trip's message comes clear – remember the journey, relish the journey. It is given not as a guide for the times when we're out traveling but for the time spent at home. As far as anyone here can say for sure, this, right now, is all the time that you or me or any of us have got. So cherish it. Be in it. Make it great and keep making it better.

We can try all we want to save an hour, but we cannot get back the days we squander.

October 28, 2001

INDEX

About the Author

Ron Colone's preferred vehicle of expression is the short essay. Ron generally writes about a dozen essays a month. He usually writes at night.

Index

Printed in the United States
3218